LEFT FOR
DEAD

BY:

Ebony Canion

Life Changing Books in conjunction with Power Play
Media
Published by Life Changing Books
P.O. Box 423 Brandywine, MD 20613

Library of Congress Cataloging-in-Publication Data;

www.lifechangingbooks.net
13 Digit: 978-1934230596
10 Digit: 1934230596

I dedicate this book to my four children:
Darnell Jr., Darnez, Dariell and Shawn Jr.,
who gave me strength when none could be found.

ACKNOWLEDGEMENTS

I have to first thank My Lord and Savior Jesus Christ, boy oh boy you are the best at what you do. You have a way of showing up and doing your thing and I'm forever grateful for your unconditional love, and the arms that you kept open for me when I went astray! You never held what I'd done against me, and for wiping my slate clean. You are an Almighty God and I'm thankful for the strength and wisdom you've given me, and the courage to share my story. I hope I'm making you proud! I love you Lord and I'm honored to be your vessel!

To my children, I thank you all for the pauses in your lives that you have taken in order for mine to continue on play. You all have been by my side the whole time and I thank you Darnell, Darnez, Shawn & Dariell. We have been through a lot but yet we still stand with our heads up. I love you guys for giving me more than enough reasons to keep my head up!

To my mother Rose, Ma I know I was one crazy teenager and didn't hear you when you were looking out for my best interest, but I want you to know that those words did stick with me and they have made me into the woman I am today. I thank you for the countless days that you stood with me, holding me up when my legs weren't strong enough. I love you, Ma!

I also want to thank my siblings, Troy, Charmaine and India who bonded together and formed a quilt of comfort for me. Thank you Troy for always giving me words of wisdom and encouragement, Peewee

(Charmaine) for having my back through everything, and India for not being afraid to tell me to get it together and being my ears to listen and shoulders to cry on. I can't forget my sister from another mother, Dee Dee, I love, love, love you all.

I want to thank my good friend Shannon for those words encouragement, and each day that you pushed me to fight! Words can't explain how blessed I am to have you in my life! Love you Shan.

To the entire Aikens family, also known as Grams Crew, I thank you for all your support and prayers. We are mighty when we all stand together and I'm proud to be a part of such a wacko yet loving family lol!

I have to also thank my Aunt San, Auntie you stepped in and haven't stepped out since. I love you for all that you have done for my children and me.

To the Currie, Zaid, and Canion families, I thank each and every one of you all for the prayers you said for me, and every word of encouragement you gave me, as well as my friends who stood by my side. You all are locked in my heart and will forever be a part of me.

To my loved ones who now reside in heaven: my loving husband Darnell. Baby, I love you, and I hope I'm making you proud as I do both of our parts as a parent. To my spirit building father, Marshall, Daddy look at your Mamma Pooh she's helping people like she always wanted to and remembering each word you told me about God along the way! Love you Daddy. To my nurturing grandmother, hey Gram! I know I didn't get a chance to say good-bye but that's okay because there never was a goodbye to be said, only I'll see you in a bit. I love you, Gram, and I hope I'm making you smile up there.

I want to thank my nurses, doctors and therapists who tapped into their God-given gifts and got me to where I am now! My nurses were my caregivers yet my second family, always giving me encouraging words and a good laugh everyday! You guys have no idea how much I love you all and will never ever forget you! My doctors who used their talent and put me back together like Humpty Dumpty honey! I thank you all so much! My therapists, who refused to back off me, and gave me the will to keep fighting. I thank you all as well and you'll forever be in my heart!

Naturally Gifted Fitness Center in Cleveland, Ohio for their contribution getting me back on my feet, giving me my first opportunity to speak publicly about my story, and helping me realize that speaking is indeed my purpose! I'm forever grateful.

Now, I have to thank the crew that made my book possible.

Azarel, Tressa, Ms. CEO of Life Changing Books herself, I thank you for giving me the opportunity to share my story with the world and for doing your part in God's will for my life. You are not just a publisher, you're an amazing soul and I'm blessed to know you.

Jackie, who did the photography, your work is absolutely amazing! Kim Lee—who beat this face up and raised money to help my children and me during my time of need. Kia and Greg—the videographers who put my story in action. Kelli, cover designer; Tam, stylist; Keisha George, hair stylist; Necole, behind the scenes project manager; and Tiffani from Embrace Life Media for inspiring the title.

Also, to anyone in my life who has regrets about any situation that has affected me, I'm okay and this book is for you!

Peace and Blessings,
Ebony Canion
Follow me on Instagram & Twitter: @survival_story

LEFT FOR DEAD

June 30, 2012. That night, I felt in my soul that something wasn't right. I knew going out wasn't a good idea, but it was my birthday, and my daughter, Dariell, had practically twisted my arm to go. She kept telling me over and over again that I deserved a night for myself. My gut instinct screamed, *Don't go!*, but I ignored it. I felt I deserved to go out too, and my daughter's insistence only reassured me.

So I went.

I left the house for a girl's night out. But as enjoyable as the night was, I had this dark, eerie feeling that I couldn't explain. In hindsight, I now know it was a sixth sense warning me that something was about to change my life forever.

I remember leaving the club right after the last call. My sister, India, and my cousins, Dominique and Demetria, were with me. We were all tipsy, laughing, and enjoying ourselves as we climbed into the car and headed back to my sister's house. The night had been more than fun, and I wanted to go home. But, no one wanted to take me until later. Since I wasn't driving, I had to go with the flow.

With the music playing, we turned off of Kinsman Avenue and onto my sister's street. As we approached India's driveway, we noticed a car parked in her spot. We didn't recognize the car, and had no idea why it was there. As we reached the end of the driveway, we could see four or five people sitting in the car. They appeared to be girls.

Dominique needed to pull into the driveway, so she blew the horn. We could see movement inside, but the car's driver refused to back out. Dominque continued to blow the horn, and we all started to yell at the car. The driver still didn't move.

Inside our car, we all said a few things—some rational words and some more cruel. The girls simply wouldn't leave. Dominique drove two houses down to our grandmother's house to park the car for the time being.

We got out of the car and headed down the sidewalk to India's house, approaching the car in the driveway. As we walked down the street, I knew things could get ugly. Was this why I felt the urge to stay at home with my children? Whatever the case, it was way too late. I continued walking, calming myself down, and thinking, *You gotta be the one to keep this calm.*

Strangely, after our constant urging them to leave, they backed out of our driveway.

"Thank you!" India shouted to them, annoyed.

An even stranger thing happened next. The car had
backed out of India's driveway, and into a driveway of
the house directly across the street, facing us. Suddenly
someone in the car shouted, "Fuck you, bitch. I'll beat
your ass!"

We were all caught off guard by it. Needless to say,
we shouted back to them. The car doors opened quickly,
and all five girls hopped out. It was then that India
recognized one of them as her son's father's girlfriend.
She and India had been having major issues with one
another since earlier in the year.

"You know what it is, bitch!" the girlfriend yelled.

We were all surprised by the argument that quickly
began. Needless to say, things escalated rapidly. The fuse
had been lit. Everyone met in the middle of the street
and began taunting each other. Words flew back and
forth. Then, out of nowhere, one of the girls from the
car punched me. Out of pure reflex, I swung back, even
though I didn't want any problems. I'd been through
enough pain in life already.

Then, all hell broke loose.

We were brawling in the middle of the street.
Punches and kicks were thrown in every direction. After
a bunch of yelling and name calling, the girls headed
back to their car. Both groups made threats, but only out
of anger. The girls finally rushed back into their car.
Seconds later, one of them threw a bottle from the car
window, targeted at me. It missed, shattering in the
street.

The moment that followed changed my life and will
haunt my dreams until the day I die. It was at that
moment that I realized why I had such a bad feeling

3

about going out that night. It was the reason I didn't feel right about leaving my four children at home. Things were over, and everyone had fought it out. I never expected what happened next.

The car engine revved. A second later, it sped out of the driveway, screeching and burning rubber. As it did, the driver purposely jerked the steering wheel in my direction, although she had plenty of space to go in any direction she wanted. As the headlights bore down on me, in a split second, I saw the many flashes of pain in my life: the day my father moved out, the man forcing me to do sexual things to him at a young age, the stench of the man who'd raped me in that bathroom at fourteen, the fists of the man I once loved crashing into my face, the knife intentionally forced into my mother's chest, the day I became a widow with three children to feed...

Each moment blazed by in blinding flashes, and the pain of each rushed past me. I guess it was a defense mechanism though, an act to instantly prepare me for the pain I was about to face. The car slammed into me. Immediately, the force made me crumple over the hood and my hands slammed down on its surface.

From that moment on, everything went dark for me.

My sister recalls everything that happened next. She said the car mowed me down like a racecar headed to the finish line. One moment I was there, and the next I was gone. It was like I had vanished. It happened so fast, in an absolute instant. No one watching could grasp what had happened. Even India didn't believe that I'd actually been hit.

At this point, my family had come outside. Pandemonium ensued. Everyone began to let out the most ear-piercing, horrific screams India had ever heard. But, she said the scream that affected her most was our nephew's.

"My Auntie!" he screamed. "My Auntie's under the car!"

That was when India's mind cleared, and she could decipher what just happened. The car had run me over. Along with the rest of my family, she ran out into the street as the car headed up the block. Its engine was revving loudly. Heavy smoke billowed from the hood. The gas pedal was obviously pressed to the floor, but the car moved slowly. Apparently my body, pinned underneath, slowed it down.

Even as everyone screamed in the streets, the driver of the car still didn't stop. She continued to press forward, dragging my body. It was the most horrifying sight my sister had ever seen. Finally, the car reached the corner and made a right turn. As it did, my body tore loose from the undercarriage. It flipped and rolled limply over in the street a few times and finally came to rest.

The car sped off.

My family reached me in a brief second. Although everything had happened so fast, the experience seemed to happen in slow motion. When they reached me, they couldn't believe what they saw.

I was lying on the ground with my arms and legs twisted in unnatural positions. It was obvious my bones were broken. Parts of my dress had been ripped. The jagged edges of my bones poked through my flesh. One of my legs touched my back. Patches of hair were ripped from my skull. Portions of my flesh were ripped open. Most of the left side of my face had been torn away. My tongue was ripped from my mouth and dangling. Blood spilled from me incessantly. A gory, crimson trail led from India's house to where I was lying, motionless. At that moment, everyone had the same thought. I had been literally…

LEFT FOR DEAD.

❧ CHAPTER 1 ❧

FOLLOW YOUR INSTINCTS

There will be times in life when your instincts will warn you. You get that mysterious gut feeling that often turns out to be right. Trust and follow your instincts because the potential consequences of not doing so could be detrimental or even deadly.

Ebony's Life Lesson #2

SHATTERED TRUST

Cleveland Ohio, born and raised. It's where I grew up, and experienced more turmoil and pain than most can imagine. By the time I turned thirty, I'd already died over a hundred times on the inside. Life seems to have that effect on me. See, the ironic thing about life is although it's a blessing, a true gift from God, sometimes it can feel a whole lot more like a curse. Life has definitely baptized me by fire, a harsh baptism that began smoldering me as a child. One of those bitter points of baptism came at only nine years old.

As a child, I lived with my mother and my sister, Charmaine, who was a year younger than me. My brother, Latroy, was five years older, but he didn't stay at home often. He spent most of his days with my maternal grandmother, the matriarch and savior of the family. They both came by often though. It was clear that my mother and I needed family support. My father had been absent from the house for about a year and a half. Not because he wanted to be, but because he'd been thrown out of the house.

Throughout our struggles, we still remained a tight-knit family. Even though things were unstable, I loved my family. They were my everything. Living on the eastside of Cleveland in a three bedroom, two-family house, I assumed we were living well. Of course, now that I'm older, I know we could barely make ends meet. I guess that's the wonder of childhood. As a kid, you turn each problem into play. Struggle can stare you directly in the face but you don't know it. Your innocence prevails.

My mother became a single parent after my father left. She worked hard finding work wherever she could, and went back to school hoping to become a nurse's assistant.

Despite how hard she worked, there was never enough food to get us through the month, even with the help of welfare. Usually around the middle of the month, she wouldn't eat. She'd make sure a plate was on the table for my sister and me, but she rarely ate. Back then, I didn't quite know why. When I'd ask her, she'd just say she wasn't hungry. It wasn't until years later that I realized she was choosing to go without eating because our food supply was low. This gave me my first revelation of just how much a mother would sacrifice for her children and just how much strength a mother had to have.

My mother, a sweet woman, never did drugs and rarely drank. I can count on one hand the number of times I've heard my mother say a curse word in my entire life!

My father, as far back as I can remember, wasn't much of a financial help. He didn't work, and only received a small check from the Coast Guard after being hurt and honorably discharged for saving a life. My father made up for what he couldn't do for us financially with love.

He stayed about twenty minutes away in the projects, a place that seemed to be a step down from where we were living. But in actuality, it wasn't. The ghetto was the ghetto. Drug dealers and prostitutes were on all its corners. During my many visits, I thought nothing of it. I loved visiting my father, and didn't realize the circumstances.

I did know that he and Latroy didn't click at all. Their relationship wasn't genuine like the one my dad had with Charmaine and me. Because I was nine, I was shielded from the reality that my father was on drugs. The same drugs that caused my mother to give up on their relationship. The same drugs that caused my father to live a substandard life. Still, I loved being with him. And strangely, I preferred him not with my mother. All they did was fuss and argue when they were together.

The verbal abuse my father used to inflict on my mother remains vivid in my mind. Each incident was heartbreaking. No matter what she did or said to try and make him happy, he always seemed to reward her by yelling and calling her out of her name. This would send her into a depressed state, and we never understood why.

The very first time I saw any negativity occur between my parents, I was in the room asleep with my sister, and heard my father yelling loudly. It woke me up, and caused me to peek out of the door to see what the commotion was about. I couldn't even tell what the argument was about because their words were muffled.

My father pushed my mother against the wall, and raised his hand as if he was going to strike her. I couldn't believe it! The argument grew louder as I looked back to make sure my little sister wasn't witnessing our hero becoming the villain. As I turned back to see what would happen next, I saw my brother fly out his room and lunge towards my father. Luckily, my mother grabbed him before he could reach my father. Still, my brother managed to give him a huge piece of his mind. My father walked away with his head hung low, ashamed.

My emotions were tangled. I was sad, angry, and confused, but at the same time, I was happy that Charmaine didn't see any of it. I just couldn't understand how someone could do this, someone who'd always protected us. He was my hero and my young heart was crushed! Shortly after, she finally found the courage to make him leave. I felt weird about that since most families in our neighborhood still had two-parent households.

Our street was a dead end, so everybody knew each other and they talked. It was mortifying to know that the whole street knew my parents were getting a divorce. But, life moved on and my mother seemed happier instantly.

After putting my father out, she began dating a man I will call Joe, for now. Joe was a neighbor who lived across the street and a man I'd gotten to know just from being in the neighborhood. A typical Clevelander, he

drank, had a basic job, and loved to party. He seemed
cool and used to come around often. I loved the fact
that he had children around my age, adding to the fun
times Charmaine and I shared. We spent countless
weekends with Joe and his children when they came over
to visit. I can remember my mother being really happy
during their dating phase. He genuinely seemed to care
for her and vice versa.

Shortly after we met Joe, I was surprised to see him
moving his stuff in. Although I didn't have any problems
with him, it felt weird having him move in so quickly. It
felt like he was invading what was supposed to be *our*
space; the space that my mother, sister, and I shared. Of
course my vote didn't count. It was my mother's
decision, so I had no choice but to accept it. Besides, as I
said, Joe seemed cool.

Since my mother worked a lot and went to school,
Joe was working odd jobs with different hours from my
mother's. The job market in Cleveland was horrible, so
he was home most of the time.

In all honesty, with Joe, we seemed more like a
family than we did when my mother was with my father.
Although we were struggling financially, we found ways
to have family outings such as going to the movies,
taking trips, going out to dinner, and even a trip to
King's Island, an amusement park near Cincinnati.

Our trips to King's Island were an annual family
tradition. My grandmother would come, along with my
Aunt Diane, Uncle John, Aunt Debbie, Uncle Butchie
and their children. We went every single year. It was a
chance for the entire family to get away from Cleveland
and any problems we were facing. I absolutely loved

these trips! We would stay in the hotel for a couple of days, go to the park, and then head back home.

When life was good, it was really good. But there was still struggle. Joe wasn't able to contribute a lot of money, so food still wasn't plentiful. I didn't go without though. Neither did Joe. My mother, the true provider that she was, would make sure we ate even when she didn't.

With all the ups and downs during that year, Joe's armor began to crack, and the person he *really* was became more apparent. His drinking increased and his drug problem was soon revealed to my mother. Both addictions had a hold on him that I couldn't understand back then. One minute he was cool, the next he was a stranger. He began pawning stuff around the house on a regular basis, causing us to lose items we loved, such as the television and stereo. I hated that I couldn't watch cartoons, or listen to music. For as long as I could remember, I had always loved music. "Reasons" by Earth, Wind & Fire was my jam back then. But without a stereo, the music was gone.

A quick, downward spiral began. Joe also became abusive towards my mother. He'd come in and snap on her without any given reason. Now I know what his reason was: with everything pawned, no job, and money already being scarce around the house, his addiction would flare up, and there was no way for him to get high. He would basically be feenin' so bad to get high it would send him into a rage. He'd be so angry that he'd call my mother names and yell at her. Eventually though, the abuse surpassed the name-calling. He began to abuse her, and it happened even when he wasn't feenin'.

A lesson was being taught to me, one that adolescence, naivety, and immaturity couldn't allow me to understand. The only thing you can trust about life and people is that at any given time, one of the two will always hurt you. My mother was living proof. She'd trusted my biological father, her husband, and things didn't work out. She trusted Joe, and he was now hurting her every chance he got too.

None of us are immune to that lesson. Not even a child. I didn't realize it until one of the people I thought I could trust betrayed me in the most horrendous way that a child could ever experience.

Like most kids at nine years old, I was bony, knock-kneed, had no breasts, and no shape. I was pretty much a beanpole. There was absolutely nothing about my shape that could compare or compete with the shape of a grown woman. That's why I'll never understand why or how a close family member could find interest in doing the things he did to me.

The first time he did it was one day while my mother was gone. No one else was around. I still remember sitting on the couch while he sat in this huge, orange recliner chair. That chair always seemed humungous to me, probably because I was so small back then.

"Come here, Ebony," he told me.

I didn't know what he wanted. But as a child, I was taught that you didn't back talk an adult or ask questions. When they told you to come, you came. End of story.

I got up from the couch and walked over to him. When I reached him, he stared at me for a moment. I didn't know why. A moment later, his hand was

13

underneath my shirt, rubbing my small breasts and playing with my nipples.

I had no clue why he was doing it. He'd never done that to me before. I had no idea how to react or what to say. Something inside told me it wasn't right, but I sat there. I was terrified and confused. I had always hidden myself when changing my clothes, and now this man saw what I'd tried hard to hide. He saw my young body, and there was nothing I could do about it.

Why was the man I trusted making me feel so funny inside? This wasn't the happy feeling that I had with him before. It was a feeling that I had never felt towards any other human being. I would soon figure out that it was disgust.

He grabbed my hand, placed it on the crotch of his pants and told me to rub him. As he pulled his penis out, I was sick to my stomach. I had never seen anything so ugly in my life! But even though I felt disgusted, I continued to do what he'd told me.

I can't explain how dirty and shameful I felt. All I knew was I didn't like it, so I detached myself from what was happening while I followed his lead. I let my young mind drift off to other thoughts; anything that would distract me from what he was making me do.

Eventually he let me stop, telling me, "And don't you say nothing to nobody, 'cause ain't nobody going to believe you."

Unable to even process his words, I silently went back to the couch and sat down glassy-eyed, staring off into mid-air. My instinct told me to tell my mother, but I allowed his words, "Ain't nobody going to believe you," to manifest in my soul. In all honesty, I just wanted to forget that it happened.

I had to hide what happened to me from Charmaine too. I was both ashamed and afraid that if I told her and word got out, I would be the one to get in trouble. My only hope at that moment was that it would stop. Little did I know, my molester had other intentions that would leave *this* moment, and several more like it, etched in my brain forever.

It didn't take long for him to strike again. It was less than a month later. My feelings had changed from bewilderment to anger. The routine was set—same place, same orange chair, and the same instructions.

Even though I didn't resist, I didn't do things exactly as he said. There was more resentment from me during the second incident. From the onset of the last attack on my innocence, I wanted so badly to tell my father, knowing he would protect me. One thought was that he'd take me away, allowing me to live with him. Another thought was that he'd show up and beat that bastard to a pulp for hurting me. But faster than I could concoct those thoughts, they would disappear after hearing his words resonate in my brain, "Ain't nobody going to believe you."

So, against my gut feeling, I kept it all to myself, not feeling comfortable with exposing what was happening to me. Thoughts of telling my mother or grandmother were considered and then quickly discarded.

Still, he wouldn't stop. The incident occurred again. And just like the others, it didn't last long. But this time was the last time he touched me and forced me to touch him. To this day, I don't know why it stopped. I was

15

relieved and felt as if I had received my childhood back. I could finally be a kid again. I simply wanted to go outside with my friends and play, to be a normal kid, and not thrown into a world where things were being done to me that I knew weren't right. No child should have to worry like I did.

I have my speculations on why he stopped, but we've never discussed it. All that remains are speculations and secrets that I carried with me for years, killing me on the inside.

❧ CHAPTER 2 ❧

UPGRADE YOUR WORTH

Self worth is the key to living a life with your head held high. When you think less of yourself you tend to accept an unexceptional quality of life. Value yourself highly no matter the circumstances. Accepting mediocre treatment is not an option. Love yourself enough to live a better life. You determine how others treat you.

Ebony's Life Lesson #3

A TASTE OF TROUBLE

Many different faces come in and out of our lives at different times for different reasons. Some are good, some are bad. Some faces bring joy and give you a reason to wake up each morning. Other faces make you despise and regret the very moment you first crossed paths with them.

One of my favorite faces, my sister India's, came into my life on September 29, 1987. Being Charmaine's big sister didn't have the same effect on me since we were only a year apart. But, I could take care of India—change her diapers, pick her up, and play house. She was adorable. She had the fattest cheeks and always brought joy to the atmosphere.

By the time India was a year old, my mother would let me and Charmaine help out with things such as dressing her, feeding her, and pushing her in her stroller. We loved it. I was madly in love with my baby sister.

Like I said before, being the big sister was like a badge of honor to me. It made me want to stick my chest out and show I could handle the title.

Despite the happiness India brought, her presence also brought problems. The money situation in our house wasn't any better. Our mother was still working hard, but during this period, Joe still wasn't working. Looking back on it, in all honesty, I really don't think he was genuinely putting any effort into finding another job. My mother was taking care of him and he'd gotten used to it. So with only one source of income, the addition of India, and both Charmaine and I constantly growing out of our shoes and clothes, money grew scarcer. I guess one can imagine how many headaches and the amount of stress that caused. One of the people that eased the problems was my grandmother.

My grandmother was a godsend. When things got tough, she could always be depended on to come through. She loved my mother and her grandbabies, so there was pretty much never a moment of need when she didn't at least offer her help. She was already taking on most of the responsibilities for Latroy since he lived with her, but she always had my back, too.

One of my favorite memories of my grandmother coming through in a bind was when I was in the sixth grade, preparing to graduate to junior high. I was so excited. But since money was short, neither my mother nor father could afford to buy me a dress. I still remember my mom sitting me down and saying, "I might not be able to get your dress for you for graduation." My heart was broken. Tears ran down my face.

One of the things about that moment that also hurt me was the look on my mother's face when she broke the news to me. The pain of not being able to afford to give me what I needed at such an important point in my life hurt her beyond measure. It was all over her face. I'd seen that pain in her before. There were countless times when despite her hard work, she couldn't afford to give us the things we wanted or that she wanted us to have. It upset her deeply each time. This time though, the pain seemed to cut her deeper than the others. But, in all honesty, like most ten year olds, despite my mother's hurt, I thought more about my desires at that moment. I wanted what *I* wanted. That dress.

Seeing my tears, hurt, and disappointment, my mother said, "Ebony, don't cry. I'll ask your grandmother. You'll have a graduation dress."

I knew my grandmother could always be depended upon. This time though, she made me nervous. Time began to wind down and she still hadn't come through. The friends I socialized with at school were all discussing their new dresses. I couldn't join in the conversation. I began to worry more and more as each day passed. Eventually, I figured that I wouldn't get the dress. But, the day before graduation, my grandmother called and told my mother to have me ready because she was on her way to get me. She only lived five minutes away. The five minutes on that particular day though felt like five years.

I wasn't sure why my grandmother was coming. Since it was only a day before graduation, I was worried that maybe she was coming to tell me she couldn't get the dress. It was a nerve-racking wait. Finally, she pulled

19

up. When she came in the house, I asked her where we were going.

In her soft voice, she said, "We're going to May Company to get your dress."

I screamed at the top of my lungs with excitement. I jumped and danced doing my famous jiggle that my family loved to see me do. When we left my house and finally arrived at May Company, I rocked the biggest smile imaginable on my face. My smile was so huge and animated that I couldn't conceal it. I thanked her over and over again.

"Don't worry, baby," she told me. "That's what I'm here for."

I really don't know what my family would have ever done without my grandmother during that time. Her presence and assistance proved to be priceless.

Needless to say, I headed into junior high school at the start of the next school year. I was beyond excited. My friends and I always used to talk about how it would be. We couldn't wait to see what it would be like to have lockers and multiple classes instead of having to sit in one classroom all day like in elementary. Also, junior high made us feel grown up. Inside, I really was maturing.

Salt-N-Pepa was *super* hot at the time. They were the female version of Run DMC. We loved them. I loved them so much that I dressed and rocked my hair like them. I chose to look like Salt. I had a short bob with blonde ends and you couldn't tell me we weren't twins. I wanted to rap and be just like her!

Junior high proved to be a lot of fun for me. I met new friends, experienced new things, and loved it all. I was even an honor student. But just like any stage in life, a person encounters some things that aren't quite in their best interest. Sometimes people find themselves affected by their surroundings. I'm not exempt. My surroundings began to swallow me up, and I didn't put up a fight. This was one of those stages for me.

A moment that I will never forget occurred at home instead of school. Although my experience in junior high was going well, things at home weren't. Since our financial position hadn't changed, my mother and Joe argued more than before. This particular time though, the arguing turned into something much more lethal and tragic.

Charmaine and I were in the house having fun when Joe and my mother came home. My mother had gotten pregnant again, even though India was just a year old. As time went by, a friend of Joe's came by. The two friends headed down to the basement. Moments later, my mother went down to the basement, too. Suddenly an argument broke out between Joe and my mother. This argument was a little different than the others because my mother was actually arguing back.

My mom is the strongest woman I know, and she never liked to argue. I hate to call her meek, but that's how God made her. She was petite, and always seemed to stay quiet or say as little as possible during the arguments. This time was different though. She was eight months pregnant and had already named the child in her womb Taylor Marie.

The argument began because my mother had gone downstairs and caught Joe, and his friend, smoking crack. It sent her into a fury and sent them all running upstairs. The shouting match had become more spiteful than I'd ever witnessed before. Charmaine and I crept from our bedroom to watch it all unfold.

"No, Joe!" she yelled angrily. "Get him out of my house!"

Joe shrugged her off.

"Joe, I'm not playing. Get him *out*. If you don't, you can leave too!"

That's when things got crucial.

Not taking too kindly to the ultimatum, Joe yelled back, "If you wouldn't have brought your nosy muthafuckin' ass down here, you wouldn't know what the hell we were doing."

"This is my house, Joe. I don't want that stuff in here. If you can't deal with that, you can go!"

My sister and I peeked around the corner and that was when he pushed her, knocking her face down on the ground. Before that moment, Joe's abuse had been mostly verbal, like my biological father's had been. This was the first time he had hit her, or at least this was the first time Charmaine and I had witnessed physical abuse. At the time, I had no idea about all the mental abuse my mother had been enduring.

I fumed, angry inside, and waited for my mother to punch him back, yet she didn't. She laid there, crying out, holding her stomach. As if she was trash on the street, both Joe and his friend stepped over her and left. With tears flowing from my eyes, my sister and I rushed to help my mother. Holding her stomach, she assured the two of us that she was okay. Eventually though, we discovered otherwise. After an hour passed, she cried out in pain and began bleeding. She then called my grandmother, told her that she'd fallen down the steps, and needed a ride to the hospital.

"Don't lie to me," my grandmother said sternly through the phone. She knew something wasn't right. She'd seen through Joe a long time ago.

"I fell down the steps," my mother continued.

"Tell me what really happened." My grandmother refused to let it go. She demanded the truth. Finally my mother broke down and admitted Joe had beaten her.

"That no good sucka," my grandmother said. "I knew it."

It didn't take my grandmother long to arrive at the house. She took my mother to the emergency room. Later on, she took us back to her house where we spent the night away from Joe.

The next day, my mother called us. Happy to hear her voice, I asked how she was doing.

"I'm okay," she said in low voice.

"How's Taylor Marie? Is she okay?"

There was a deafening silence, one I will always remember.

"Ma?"

This time I heard sniffling and light crying from my mother's end of the phone.

"She didn't make it," she finally said in a distressed tone.

Hearing her crying, I wished so badly that I could take her grief away. I wished there was a way I could make her feel better. It was killing me, and hurt me to the core. This was my mother, and I couldn't bear hearing the pain in her voice. The sweetest woman I knew was filled with hurt, and I couldn't do anything about it.

"Momma, don't cry," I said. "It's going to be okay. I love you."

"I love you, too."

And that was it.

Taylor Marie was gone.

Until this day, I still wonder what it would have been like to know her. I wonder what she would have become. It was at that moment that life taught me another one of its harsh lessons— how to deal with grief. Maybe He was preparing me for the tough road ahead. Despite how badly it hurts when you lose the ones you love, life goes on.

The good Lord is always in charge. He knows best and determines our future.

* * *

I entered the seventh grade a few months later. My social life at Alexander Hamilton Junior High had changed drastically—for the worst. My first year I was an honor student and stayed to myself only choosing to associate with a few close friends, but, in the eighth grade, something inside me changed. I guess as the older folks used to say, I had reached the age where I was beginning to "smell my piss".

I don't know what was going on with me. I just began rebelling and not taking school seriously anymore. I started hanging around with the wrong people. Eventually the change in me caused me to fail the eighth grade. I just couldn't seem to get it together. My father would give me lectures about the path I'd chosen to take in life. I was his baby and it hurt him to think about where I would end up. He asked me if I still had dreams of becoming a lawyer.

"Yes," I remembered telling him so confidently. I really did still want to be a criminal attorney. My aspirations were there, but the streets often sidetracked my plans.

I allowed my environment to pull me in knowing there was something bigger and better out there for me. My failure to get it together eventually caused me to get beat badly. One time, a friend and I were walking to visit another friend, and a group of girls walked up on us. At the time I was dressed in a pair of red and white Air Jordans and a Triple Fat Goose trench. I was in to gangbanging, unbeknownst to my family.

"What set you claimin'?" one of the girls asked.

Refusing to back down, I repped my 'hood. The problem was my friend and I were in the *wrong* 'hood. Words were exchanged, and one of the girls approached me. I knew if I let her get too close, she'd most likely steal on me. So I swung first. Before I knew it, her friends were on me like a swarm of bees. Out of nowhere, at least five people attacked me. I remember one of them being a guy. The punches were excruciatingly painful. Between the kicks to my body, my hair being pulled, and blood spilling from my body, I found myself on the ground, trying to use my arms and hands to shield my body from the blows. I could never figure out why my friend didn't jump in to help me.

I continued to fight hard, although most of my fighting was on my back as I laid on the cold winter cement. Eventually I was able to get to my feet. But, instead of continuing to fight, I took off running. I looked back to see my friend still standing on the corner. As I ran, the girls chased me, along with two other guys. I remember screaming wildly for help. I was even screaming for my momma, the same person who had warned me this would happen if I kept heading down this path.

One of the girls, who lived just five houses away from mine, grabbed me from behind. Before I knew it, I was on my back again, getting beat badly. Eventually the torture ended. I wound up going to the emergency room. There were no broken bones or a need for stitches. I mainly had bumps, bruises, and a battered ego. They whooped me so bad I had a Nike shoe print on my forehead.

I should've stopped gangbanging at that moment, especially when my friend told me that the reason she never helped me was because someone had a gun to her side the entire time. We all could have been killed, but I didn't stop. Instead, I used that moment as a lesson, and just chose to move differently so I could avoid taking a loss like that again.

Also around this time, after turning thirteen and in the eighth grade again, I began to take interest in boys. There was one in particular, a handsome, tall, slim, light-skinned dude with beautiful hazel eyes. Ironically though, he wasn't a boy technically. He was eighteen years old. He was a man. In his defense, he had no idea I wasn't eighteen too. I had lied to him. I was growing sneaky at that time.

To get close to this dude, I befriended his sister. She used to do my hair, so I used that to my advantage. One day while she was doing my hair, after she left the room to go do something, I winked at him, told him he was sexy, and asked for his number. Being molested had instilled aggressiveness in me when dealing with boys. It made me refuse to let the opposite sex take advantage of me. After exchanging numbers, the two of us began to talk a lot, but I still kept my age a secret. I also began to visit him a lot, no longer needing to use his sister to get close to him. Eventually the inevitable happened.

I can remember walking to his house that night. He only lived a few doors down from us, but the walk felt like forever. I just knew in my soul what was going to happen that evening. When I got there, no one was there but me and him. He led me to his bedroom where we sat cuddling and watching television. A while later, without saying anything, he kissed me and I loved it. It was a deep kiss, a whole lot of tongue, which my mouth savored. When he finally turned my mouth loose, moans began to leave it, as his hands explored other parts of my body. I melted in his hands. Needless to say, I was soaking wet.

Ready to give myself to him, I asked him if he had a condom. I'd learned about practicing safe sex from listening to my brother kick it with his friends. He said he did. Technically, I wasn't a virgin at the time in my head. Although I had been molested, I had never been penetrated. Of course, I had never wanted it from my molester, but I was definitely anxious to experience it now as he slid the condom on.

It didn't take long before he was inside me. There was a little pain, but it eventually became pleasure. It was good, but what totally had my attention were the noises and faces he made. My body had him acting in ways I had never seen. It was as if I weakened him. It turned me on, especially when he climaxed.

When we were done, I left. Afterwards, I didn't call him, but he began calling me on a regular basis. It was like he was absolutely *thirsty* for more of me. It was then that I realized just how powerful sex was, specifically the power of a female. It could control a man, especially if used correctly. At that moment, I realized how much I loved knowing I had that power. And like most other girls my age, I wanted more of it. I had found a way to weaken a man and I loved it! Boy, was I in for a rude awakening.

I had no idea about the tragic road I would soon travel as a teenager.

OUTSIDE INFLUENCES

One of the biggest problems with being a kid is the rush to be grown. As kids, from a distance, we see all of the perks of being grown and we want them. Our wants become so extreme that we begin to act grown ourselves, not realizing that being grown comes with a whole lot of circumstances a child isn't truly equipped to handle. I had to learn that lesson the hard way.

My mother's sister, Aunt Diane, was my favorite aunt because she always let me have my way. With her, I could be as fast and hot in the pants as I wanted to be. She and her husband, John, had given me my first drink. They smoked weed, drank, and partied a lot and had no problem allowing me to indulge, as long as I didn't tell my mother. I loved it.

One day during the eighth grade, my Aunt Diane called and said she was having a get-together. Immediately I was pumped because I knew her get-togethers were always the bomb. And of course, I'd be able to get down like a grown up.

"I'm coming over," I said, almost before she could get the entire sentence out.

After accepting the invitation, I didn't bother to tell my mother because I knew she wouldn't want me to go. Since I was already feeling myself at that time, she figured her sister would be a bad influence. She'd stoke the fires of my already increasingly bad behavior. It was getting to the point where my mother didn't even want me to leave the house.

In hindsight, I can't blame her. Now that I'm a parent, I know exactly how it feels. I wouldn't want *my* daughter leaving the house either if I saw that the outside world was beginning to corrupt her in ways that could eventually get her hurt or killed.

Anyway, I walked to my aunt's party anxious to turn up. She didn't live too far so it wasn't unusual for me to walk there. When I arrived, I realized it was just a small get-together. No one was there but her, John, and two of their friends. I was still down though. The small number of people wouldn't change the fact that my auntie would allow me to do me.

"What's up, Eb?" my Uncle John greeted me as I strolled up while he was working the barbecue grill.

"Hey, Uncle Bae Bae," I returned.

He gave me some dap on the hand and I went into the house. Inside the music was already playing. There was a table covered with bottles of liquor, which I noticed immediately. My mouth watered at the sight.

"Hey, E Double," my auntie happily greeted me by my nickname and gave me a hug.

She then introduced me to two guys. I can't remember the name of one but I *definitely* remember the name of the other. His name was Brian, and he looked to be somewhere in his mid-twenties while the other guy looked to be in his forties.

As I said, the music was already playing. While it did, everyone was already enjoying the party. Weed smoke clouded the room. I loved its smell. Just like when she'd given me my very first drink, my aunt had also given me my very first hit of weed. I now smoked with her often during her social gatherings and I couldn't wait to smoke with her at the current moment.

I looked up to my auntie. She was my heart and definitely, in my opinion, the realest definition of a "Fly Chick", way before today's generation began using the term. Even though she was short, she always kept her hair and nails done. And she was always fly. Everyone knew her. She had such an influence on me. I wore eyeliner, red lipstick, and big hoop earrings just so I could look like her.

With her arms around my shoulders, over the loud music, she asked me, "What you drinkin'?"

"Vodka with orange juice and light ice."

She hooked up my drink and I took it to the head, trying to show her and everyone around I was grown. With that, I began my evening. My aunt and I, and her two friends, began to converse about anything and everything. Uncle John came in occasionally to grab a drink, crack a few jokes, and then returned to the grill. Time was passing and I was enjoying myself while drinking beer and liquor, and growing more and more intoxicated. Of course I was hitting the joint my auntie kept in constant rotation. At that point I had never felt so mature.

As the music played, we all sang along to each song in drunken harmony. I can remember my aunt's forty-something-year-old friend jokingly saying the rest of us were too young to know anything about the songs we were singing. By this time, my uncle had come in from working the grill and had joined the party full time.

As everything was happening, I gravitated towards Brian, the twenty-something-year-old, and began to spark up a conversation with him. I asked him everything from where he lived to where he worked, trying to sound as ladylike and worldly as possible. In all honesty, although only fourteen at the time, my conversation was on his level.

"How do you know my aunt and uncle?" I asked with a drink in my hand.

"From the neighborhood," he told me.

"Where do you live?" I asked him again.

"Right up the block on the corner."

As time passed, the two of us drifted into our own world. I asked more and more questions. No one else existed. We just talked and laughed amongst ourselves, finding enjoyment in each other's company.

"Are you seeing anybody?" he finally asked.

"No," I answered.

I knew the question was a come on, a come on that a grown man shouldn't have asked a child. But I wasn't trying to be a child in that moment. His question solidified the fact that I talked more like an adult. If anything, right then, the only thing that had me unnerved was that my aunt would hear what we were discussing and shut the whole thing down by revealing my age.

I really didn't think too much of what he'd asked, although obviously I should've. I was too busy thinking it was cute. It was just something to do. I knew that we would never date and I knew the moment wouldn't go beyond the party.

Time passed with me growing more intoxicated. Eventually we all took the party outside. The music grew louder and we all started dancing to everything from Earth, Wind & Fire to Salt- N-Pepa, Sugarhill Gang and 2Pac. As we enjoyed ourselves, I noticed Brian swerving around, wasted. He was so done that he slurred his speech and stumbled around the front yard. It seemed funny to me, especially since I was the one who was supposed to be acting that way since I was the baby of the party.

"Your drinks are cut off," I can remember telling him jokingly. "You don't need anymore."

"I agree," Uncle John cosigned.

Before long, my drinks caught up with me also. I began to feel sick.

"Your drinks are cut off too," my uncle told me, noticing how tore up I was.

Moments later, I had to urinate and possibly throw up, so I headed in the house and went upstairs to use the bathroom. Pulling my pants down and sitting on the toilet, despite how drunk I was, it crossed my mind that I was going to have to spend the night. There was no way I could go home and let my mother see me in that condition. She'd never let me come back over my aunt's house again if she saw me like this.

33

A knock sounded at the door.

"I'm in here," I said.

A few more knocks followed.

"I'm in here," I said again.

Suddenly the door sprung open and Brian's face appeared. His expression was drunkenly twisted. Even from the little distance between us, I could smell the liquor and beer radiating from his body and breath.

"You okay?" he asked in slurred speech. "I came to see if you're okay."

"Yeah, I'm good," I told him with annoyance in my voice. I was pissed at him for busting in on what was obviously a private moment. "Can't you see I'm using the bathroom? Get out."

Ignoring what I'd told him, he stumbled into the bathroom and shut the door behind him. The bathroom was tiny enough with one person. Two people made it practically a telephone booth. Quickly, I stood from the toilet and began to pull my panties and jeans up. As I got them halfway up my thighs, looking down at my crotch, he said the words that I will never forget, words no grown man should say to a child…

"What 'chu tryin' to hide that 'lil shit fo'?"

"What are you talking about?" I asked, knowing exactly what he was talking about, but too unnerved by the situation to know what else to say. He was much bigger than me and I knew exactly where the situation was headed.

The look Brian had on his face was sick. What he wanted was obvious.

"Look, Brian," I said sternly while struggling to get my clothes up. "You need to get the hell out of here right now!"

"Give me that 'lil shit," he demanded sternly.

I'll never forget the sound and tone of his voice as he said it. Remnants of the way he sounded when we were all downstairs enjoying ourselves were gone. He sounded and looked like a totally different person. I was absolutely terrified to death.

Before I could say anything else, Brian grabbed me and forced me completely around until my exposed rear was to him and my face was in the mirror. In the mirror's reflection, we were eye to eye. It had to have been obvious to him that I was scared. I knew he could see it.

"Stop, Brian!" I screamed as I struggled to turn around while also still struggling to get my clothes up. "You're drunk. Stop it!"

Ignoring me, he forced me against the sink and grabbed hold of my jeans and panties to keep me from pulling them up. I was obviously no match for his strength.

"Brian, stop it!" I screamed again while hoping someone would hear me. No one did though. The music was too loud and everyone was still outside. Finally, realizing screaming wasn't going to help, I tried another approach; I tried to talk him down. "Brian, why do you want to do this?" I asked meekly.

Ignoring me, Brian began to pull his pants down. I continued to try my hardest to talk him out of it. I spoke fast and desperate, dreading what was coming. Finally, realizing talking wasn't going to help, I pleaded, "Brian, please don't do this." Tears filled my eyes. I could barely see anymore.

"Shut the fuck up," he told me while still keeping me wedged against the sink so hard the bones of my hips were starting to ache.

Up until that moment, I had only had intercourse with one other person so I knew what was about to happen was going to hurt. Little did I know though, hurt wasn't even the word for it. Everything began to happen quickly. He shoved himself inside me with brutal force. It was the most painful feeling I'd ever felt. It felt like the inside of my vagina was being burned and ripped. The dry friction was unbearable.

"Please, Brian, stop!" I screamed in pain. "It hurts!"

Still ignoring me, he rammed inside me, breathing heavy with each thrust. All I could do was cry and hope the moment would end quickly. The pain was killing me. But just like the times I'd been molested, my mind drifted someplace else. It was the only way to deal with what was happening to me. It was the only way to deal with losing what was being taken away from me.

In hindsight, I think he may have gotten scared, or thought he heard someone coming, because he never ejaculated. He eventually stumbled backwards while pulling his pants up and said, "I told yo' 'lil ass to give me that 'lil shit."

Hearing those words and looking teary-eyed at him through the mirror, that statement played tricks with my young mind. The way he said it had me wondering had I done something to deserve this? Was it my fault I had been raped? Had I caused it? Had I acted too grown?

"You better not tell nobody," he said harshly, and staggered out of the bathroom leaving me on my own.

For a moment I thought about telling my aunt and uncle what had happened. But the words of my molester appeared inside my head. "Ain't nobody going to believe you." Hearing those words made me second-guess what, in hindsight, I should've done.

With trembling hands and while wiping countless tears away, I was confused and hurt. Had I led him on in some kind of way? Did I deserve what had just happened to me? Was it my fault? I couldn't put things into perspective and my heart was totally crushed by what had just happened. I cleaned my bleeding vagina, got myself together, and headed downstairs and onto the porch, only to discover Brian sitting off in a corner staring at me with the most evil stare I had ever come across. It was like a death stare.

"You better not tell nobody," his words played inside my head. "You better not tell nobody." The words just kept repeating. It was like he was teleporting them to me through that stare of his. I was so scared I shook continually.

Needing to get away from the moment, I simply told my aunt and uncle I was too drunk to continue partying and went upstairs to a bedroom, locked the door, and curled up into a tight ball, hoping he wouldn't attempt to come back for more.

* * *

For a while after the rape I could still feel Brian's hands on my body. I could still smell the liquor drifting from his breath. It was strange. There were moments when I could smell the stench of his body in the wind. I was even having nightmares and waking up in cold sweats, expecting to see him in the darkness of my bedroom, maybe sitting in the corner like a demon. I would hear his voice somewhere behind me at times while out somewhere, and then quickly and fearfully turn around to discover it was someone else. It was crazy. Each time made me queasy.

I wanted to tell somebody, especially my uncle John, because I knew he was super protective. I knew he'd possibly beat the hell out of Brian. But I guess I feared he wouldn't believe me. Eventually, like the molestation, I just decided to block out the rape.

As I said, there's a lot more to being an adult than a child understands or is prepared for. And trying to disguise yourself as an adult only brings its problems and situations rushing to you faster than expected.

Before long, I turned fifteen. By that time, I had blocked the rape out completely, not realizing the effect that moment had on me. Ironically, it made me promiscuous. I guess I felt that the rape, plus the fact that I'd had sex once before, had earned me stripes somehow. It licensed me to have sex freely. Strangely, I became the aggressor, refusing to allow men to have the upper hand over me.

I began to have sex with boys around my neighborhood regularly, on my own terms though. I felt like I had power over them because they always wanted seconds, but it was up to me whether I called them back or not. Now I know it was immature and ignorant. But back then I didn't know any better.

My mother, father, nor my grandmother had any idea how promiscuous I had become. They were busy working hard. I began spending a lot of time at my grandmother's house in the Kinsman area of Cleveland. Kinsman was considered middle class. Everybody knew each other. It was a 'hood where all my cousins and brother knew everyone. A lot of people were attracted to my grandmother's house because it was known to have all the teenaged, pretty girls hanging around.

To this day, I'm not sure if she knew just how popular my brother Latroy was. My grandmother would go to work leaving us all there. Knowing her schedule like clockwork, we'd clean everybody out before she came back. It was truly the party house.

Time passed and I met a guy that really caught my attention. His name was James DeShannon Davis, well known to the world as MC Brains, or just Brains. He was from our neighborhood, Union Square, and was best friends with a guy named Darnell who I knew very well. During the early nineties, Brains was signed to Michael Bivins' record label, along with BBD, Boys II Men, and Another Bad Creation. He'd found success and had become Cleveland's very *first* official platinum MC. He would come by my grandmother's house often.

I asked Darnell to hook it up so that Brains and I could sleep together, and he did. Darnell told him, and of course he accepted. It wasn't the scene I would have wanted, but it happened. We met in my grandmother's basement and it was on! We made it quick, and it was over. Of course now I know that was insane.

Shortly after, Brains started touring and my attention turned to Darnell. Everybody called him Meatball. He was a friend of my brother's and I was attracted to him instantly. He was super sexy to me. Of course I loved seeing him come to the house. Darnell was popular in the 'hood. Everyone knew him and wanted to be around him. He was like a magnet. His smile, sense of humor, style of dress, and swagger just drew people to him, and always made him the center of attention. I wanted that attention myself so it was only natural that I would want to be his girlfriend.

Darnell was much older than me and was in the twelfth grade. My mother didn't know though. I never told her out of fear she'd definitely put a stop to us. I was feeling Darnell too much, and there was no way I could have that.

The relationship between Darnell and I grew quickly. I fell in love with him. It was deep and real. I'd never felt that way before. I was feeling him so much that I began cutting school with him. When I did, we would chill at his house in his bedroom, which was the attic of his parents' home.

Of course we began having sex before long. That was the only way I knew to show love at the time. Sex with him seemed amazing, like none I'd experienced before. Darnell proved to be tender and caring towards me. His touch was always soft. His words were always loving. And his thrusts inside me were always specifically meant to give me pleasure. He'd always tell me how pretty I was. No one had ever done those things to me before, not even my father. Eventually though, our little sexcapades became embarrassingly discovered.

One day while cutting school at his house and having sex, the door burst open and his mother stormed in. Immediately Darnell tried to lie on top of me and position the covers in a way that would keep me hidden.

"Boy, what the hell you doin' home and not in school?" his mother roared.

"They sent me home," he lied.

I could barely breathe underneath Darnell. But the fact that I was suffocating was second on my mind. The first was fear. The thought of being dead wrong all up in his mother's house sent chills through my spine. All I could do was hope she wouldn't kill me if she caught me.

"Who's in that damn bed with you?" she asked, walking over to the bed.

I buried my face in Darnell's chest and started praying. It was my last defense.

The covers flew back.

Jig's up.

"What the hell?" she gasped when she saw me. "Girl, get your damn fast ass out of that bed and get your clothes on. I'm calling your mother, you little slut."

Out of embarrassment, all I could say over and over was, "I'm sorry." My biggest focus remained on trying to keep as much distance between the two of us while I dressed, so she couldn't hit me.

"What's your damn mother's number?" she asked.

I told her, too scared to lie, even though I knew my mother would kill me. As I dressed, she called my mother right in front of me. Occasionally Darnell and I made eye contact. Silently our eyes said the same thing to each other, "Sorry, baby. Wish I could help you, but I'm too busy trying to keep the fire off my *own* ass."

We all ended up downstairs in the living room where I sat on the couch waiting for my mother. That wait seemed like an eternity. It always does for a child when you know your mother is getting ready to give you some of that good, old fashioned straighten up. Finally, my mother's car pulled up. Man, I can't tell you just how hard my heart was beating. I thought it would burst from my chest. I walked outside scared to death, only to discover she wasn't in the car. Instead, it was Joe.

Why him? I wondered. We weren't tight, and at a time like that, I didn't expect him to be the one handling my situation. Hopping out of the car, Joe said, "Girl, what the hell is wrong with you? You've got your mother all upset. Get your ass in this car!"

I don't know what made me react so defiantly but I said, "No, I'm not going." Looking at me like I had lost my mind, he told me I was definitely getting in the car with him, and that my mother was waiting on me.

Unexpectedly Darnell came outside and said, "She ain't got to go nowhere!"

"Little boy, who the fuck is you?"

"Stop it," I told the both of them, not wanting Darnell's mother to come outside. She had me shook and I didn't want any problems with her. I knew I was wrong, although it felt good to finally have someone stick up for me. At that moment, there wasn't a shadow of a doubt that I was in love with Darnell.

The two went back and forth with each other for a little while longer, but I realized the inevitable. I had to go home.

Finally climbing into the passenger seat and pulling away from the curb, I watched Darnell through the window until he faded away, while Joe cursed from the driver's seat. When we got home, my mother was waiting. Obviously what's understood doesn't need to be said but I'll say it anyway

I got an old fashioned punishment.

Strangely though, it wasn't the punishment that hurt me. What hurt me most was my mother finally discovering that I truly wasn't a sweet, little virgin anymore. She'd known for a while that I was straying off the straight and narrow path, but this particular moment was beyond all that. I'd really disappointed her. And as any child knows, there's no feeling worse than the one you feel when you realize you've let your mother down.

CONSEQUENCES

Oddly, I thought the streets loved me. They're filled with betrayal, violence, murder, rape and guns, but I was having the best time of my life. Yet none of the bad things mattered as I grew into my late teens.

School had become a bore to me. There was no more enjoyment in it. There was no more challenge. I had stopped carrying books, doing homework, and attending actual classes. Everything I wanted seemed to be outside its walls, especially Darnell, so I began cutting school a whole lot more than before.

I was infatuated with Darnell. He was my baby. And in the beginning, I thought he felt entirely the same way. But eventually, I discovered I wasn't the only one in his life. He was a player like most boys at eighteen. It hurt me to discover it, but I was too in love to let him go. I was too in love to forget him. So he became a big part of why I skipped school so frequently. Since he skipped a lot, I felt like I needed to keep an eye on him. So I skipped too. Dumb on my part, I know, but as a kid we all do stupid things.

Of course since I was cutting school so much, my mom would eventually get the calls from the principal letting her know I'd deliberately missed school without her knowledge. "Why are you doing this?" she'd ask me.

As I mentioned, my mother has always been soft spoken. She didn't like to raise her voice. And shamefully, just like my father and Joe, I played on it. I'd give her any old excuse to get by. I'm not saying she believed the excuses. She's not slow by any means. But she just didn't press me on the issue. She'd accept my excuses, express her disappointment, and that would be it.

Anyway, at the time, Darnell had me hooked on him. While cutting school, I was spending a whole bunch of time with him. Since I'd discovered he was a player, and I didn't want anyone else to have him, I thought my constant presence would stop him from cheating. I thought if I gave him more sex and more attention, he wouldn't have to cheat. Yes it was naïve, but we all have to learn somehow. There's no better teacher than experience itself.

Also, I was spending a lot more time with my Aunt Diane. Hanging out with her, I began drinking a lot more. My preferred, although cheap, drinks were Cisco and Thunderbird, especially when they were mixed with Kool-Aid. I was drinking both daily.

Meanwhile, the Cleveland streets were growing more and more lethal with each passing day. Still, despite how crazy the streets had become, my neighborhood, Union

Square, seemed like a close-knit community, at least to me. It was the type of community where a woman could take another woman's man but the two of them would be right back friends later on. Unfortunately, that type of betrayal was staring me directly in the face and I couldn't even see it.

By this time, school had become unbearable. I wasn't going, period. I wasn't even checking into homeroom. I had just totally lost all interest in the experience. My mother tried her hardest to make me go, even choosing to drive me there every morning. It was a valiant attempt, but I'd simply walk in the front door waving good-bye to her, then head out the back door to either run the streets or hangout with Darnell. It finally got to the point where I just wanted out of school all together, so once again I played on my mother's kindness.

"The gangs are getting too bad, Mom," I remember telling her the first day I decided I wanted to drop out.

Yes, the gang problem in Cleveland was getting worse. The movie *Colors* and the lyrics of NWA's songs had affected Cleveland just like nearly every other inner city in America. All the teenagers wanted to be gangsters. They were all selling drugs and toting guns, but it hadn't gotten as bad as I tried to make my mother believe. The way I described the gang problem to her was nothing short of the Wild Wild West. I embellished and exaggerated a lot to make it seem like I was just too scared to go to school.

I'm not sure if my mother believed me. All I can remember was her saying, "You're going to regret dropping out when you get older. Education is a very important thing. And a ninth grade education will get you nowhere."

"I know," I told her, not really wanting to hear it. Like any other teenager, I didn't take those words too seriously. I thought I knew everything.

In the meantime, Darnell had dropped out of school also. Now that I had dropped out, I assumed the both of us could spend nearly every waking moment with each other. What a birdbrain move, huh? I was truly expecting to build a future with him. I was just that amazingly in love with him.

Eventually, after countless calls from my school telling my mother I hadn't attended, she went on ahead and signed the papers to withdraw me. I knew it broke her heart but at the time, all I could think about was what *I* wanted.

My father wasn't as easygoing about the situation as my mother. He was furious with me. Before that moment, I had told him several times that I wanted to be a lawyer when I grew up. I really meant that. After going through the molestation and seeing my mother go through the things she was going through, I felt like as a lawyer I'd be able to make a difference in someone's life or situation. But once I dropped out, that put an end to the dream. And my father expressed it loudly and profanely.

"You're too smart, Ebony, and messing up your dreams isn't good. You should've stayed in school and worked hard. You would've made a great attorney." Now that I had walked away from my best chance to make it happen, he was super angry with me. I weathered the storm though. I dealt with the yelling and cussing until it eventually faded.

And just like that, life went on.

Without school, I felt literally like shackles had been taken off of my ankles. With no school to hinder me, I began partying a lot. Every day was a party. I even got a fake ID and started hitting the bars, especially The Black Velvet. It was nothing more than a hole in the wall but it was my spot!

Life became a blur at that point. I stayed drunk and high. I was constantly having sex. I was forever spending nights out. I was discovering life. I was discovering *everything* the streets and the city had to offer and loving every moment of it. Eventually though, refusing to give up on me, my mother sent me to live with my Aunt Lizzie.

I don't want to call Aunt Lizzie a Jesus freak, but that's what most people would consider her. And these days, I feel the same way she does about God. Back then, she was always saying stuff like, "Everything is possible with God" and "You can do better with God in your life." She was heavy into it.

My aunt lived in a better environment and gave me the break from the streets as my mother intended. She was a caregiver and her patients lived in her house with her. Her patients were a far different group of people than I was used to being around.

Life became much different for me while living with Aunt Lizzie. I couldn't sleep as long as I wanted. She preferred to teach me responsibility. She had me reading the Bible, cooking breakfast, and helping out with her residents. She also had me accompanying her and the residents to church.

Church back then seemed weird to me. I felt like a heathen. I felt like a hypocrite. And because of my promiscuity, I felt dirty and sinful. The inner walls made me feel like church wasn't the place for me. Aunt Lizzie knew how I felt, so she always prayed for me.

The fact that I wasn't the niece Aunt Lizzie thought I was also made me feel guilty, especially in church. Whenever her back was turned, I was sneaking a guy in her house or leave to drink, party, and do the things my mother had tried to shield me from. Although Aunt Lizzie's house was in a better area, I found a way to bring the 'hood to me.

Around this time, I began to fool around with another guy because Darnell's player ways were getting the best of me. I began to feel if he can do it, I can do it, too. And as usual, the new guy I got with was older than me. I don't know what it was back then about older men. I just couldn't help being attracted to them.

Back at home Charmaine was also experiencing the trials and tribulations of growing up. At fifteen, she was pregnant and serious about the child's father. Knowing that a baby would be too much of a responsibility, I tried to convince my mother not to let her have the baby. I was immature and making terrible mistakes obviously, but I knew a baby at fifteen wasn't a good plan. I didn't want to see my little sister end up dropping out of school too.

While my sister was pregnant, I moved back home. Darnell and I began talking again. Despite being with someone else at that time, I couldn't stay away from him.

He was my heart, although he and I broke up and got back together repeatedly, almost a dozen times. Also, he was hustling and giving me money often. That turned me on. I felt like giving me money, buying me clothes, and buying me the latest sneakers defined a man. I reveled in it. But no matter how much I loved him, there was someone else who had the power to destroy our love.

That day, I could remember calling Darnell several times. He never answered once. Immediately, I knew he was cheating. It was just a woman's intuition. I grabbed my coat and headed directly to his house. Before going, I called his cousin Dee Dee. She lived in his mother's basement. I told her I was coming to hang out with her, which wasn't uncommon. We were cool and hung out often. Obviously, I had ulterior motives this time.

After arriving at Dee Dee's, she offered me a drink. The two of us sat, talked, drank, and watched television. As we did, all I was thinking about was getting upstairs to see exactly why Darnell hadn't been answering his phone. Eventually, I couldn't take the anticipation anymore. I headed up the stairs. As I was going up, just by coincidence, he was coming down. But he wasn't alone. There was a female behind him. When I saw her face, I froze. I couldn't believe it.

It was one of my best friends.

Her eyes locked on me with fear.

With a look of surprise on his face, Darnell asked, "Ebony, what are you doing here?"

My eyes were now locked viciously on her. They were speaking to her, obviously letting her know she had a serious beating coming.

Remaining between us, Darnell said, "Ebony, it's not what you think. It's not what it looks like."

"What the fuck is she doing here?" I asked him.

"Uhh…uhh…" he managed.

That was all I needed to hear. I acted a fool in that hallway, ready to fight for my man. Before long, his mother appeared, and told us that we had to go. That was no problem to me. It was absolute music to my ears. That meant I could get her out of the house so she could take the ass whoopin' I'd been brewing for her.

Within moments of us getting outside and in the middle of the street, we were fighting for Darnell who eventually broke us up. If he hadn't, I would've killed her. After breaking us up, he surprised me by telling me he was sorry and he wanted me, not her. I should've known he was only running game, but I was in love. Like a fool, I believed him. What a mistake that turned out to be. Eventually, he cheated on me again with her!

In addition to dealing with Darnell's cheating, something else was going on. I had that gut feeling that I was pregnant.

The news knocked the air out of me. I couldn't believe it. There I was telling my sister not to have a baby at a young age, then like a fool, I went out and got knocked up. Wow.

Seventeen and pregnant.

✑ CHAPTER 5 ✑

CONTROLLING LOVE

We cannot control whom we love. The heart has a mind of its own. The heart often wears a blindfold, wandering about in search of love. And by the time the blindfold is removed, the heart refuses to let go!

Ebony's Life Lesson #6

ON MY OWN

People always say it's impossible for a woman to *not* know she's pregnant. It's a fair assessment considering there's an actual human being growing inside you. I would probably say the exact same thing if it hadn't happened to me. In all honesty I really didn't know. I had absolutely no idea.

I discovered that I was carrying a child during my fifth month of pregnancy. I didn't know mainly because I was still getting my period for those entire four or five months. It wasn't until I stopped getting it that I decided to get a pregnancy test.

The day I purchased the test from the store I was beyond scared. There isn't a word in the dictionary to explain how terrified I was of the possibility of being knocked up at such an early age. My hands shook. My heart beat more rapidly than usual, and my forehead was engulfed with sweat. Unable to face the moment alone or take the test alone, I called Darnell, knowing if I really was pregnant, it was his.

"I think I'm pregnant," I told him.

"What makes you think that?"

"I missed my period."

"You sure?"

"Yeah."

As we talked, it was obvious from his tone and the words he was using that he didn't quite believe me. How could I blame him? It was difficult for me to wrap my head around the notion of us being parents too. He agreed to come over for moral support. When he arrived, as usual, he greeted me with a kiss on the cheek with those full, luscious lips of his that I loved so much, the same lips that everyone else jokingly called "soup coolers". Even in my time of worry I was infatuated with him.

"Where's the test?" he asked.

I showed it to him hesitantly.

Shaking his head, jokingly he said, "Ohhhhh, your momma is going to kill you if it's positive."

I laughed to keep from crying. He laughed also. That was exactly what I needed at that moment. I needed his sense of humor. I needed his personality. It was those traits that always kept me attracted to him. And at that moment, I definitely needed some laughter. My fears faded for only for a few moments. A smile appeared on my face only for a minute or two. Darnell made that happen. And as he continued to make me smile, it was like I was beginning to fall in love with him all over again. I knew then that we'd always be together.

No matter how entertaining the moment became, reality slapped me back in the face. Thoughts of what my mother was going to think began to creep inside my head. Thoughts of how the neighbors would look at me started to manifest. Of course the uncertainty of how I was going to be a teenage mother while living with my own mother, and having no money or job was evident too.

With my mind filled with worries, I headed to the bathroom with the pregnancy test in my hand, dreading what I knew was coming. With each step, I felt like a convicted murderer taking her final walk down death row to the electric chair. A minute later, I was squatting over the toilet, holding the test stick underneath me with trembling hands as Darnell watched me. After urinating on the stick, shaking it off, and washing my hands, both of us looked at it together hoping we'd dodged a curveball. Our hopes were shattered immediately.

The test read positive.

All the color flushed from my face. My heart sank. I felt so disappointed in myself. Tears began to fall. Seeing my tears, Darnell quickly took me in his arms and said, "Don't worry, baby. It's all good. We're going to be alright."

I buried my face in his chest, thankful that he chose to stick by me. I'd heard the horror stories of the boys who ditched their girlfriends upon hearing they were pregnant. Darnell was now assuring me he wasn't one of them.

Taking my face softly into his hands, he jokingly told me, "I hope you're crying because you're the one who's got to tell your mother."

I laughed, not realizing at the time, the seriousness of having a child out of wedlock and at such a young age. The two of us chatted for a while. Afterward, he said he had to go, but he'd call me later. I really needed some time at that moment to think things through. After he left, I just sat on the couch in silence with millions of thoughts rambling through my head. Deep in thought, I lost track of time, not realizing it until I heard my mother's keys turning in the door. Hearing them made my heart sink again because I knew I had to tell her. Although I was turning eighteen in a few months, I still felt like a misbehaved child having to tell her.

The two of us wound up in my room where I sat on the bed with guilt, shame, and fear. Lord knows what else was written on my face. Knowing she could most likely see it, I turned away from her and broke the news. "Mom, I'm pregnant."

My mother's light skin turned a bright shade of red. "How do you know?" she asked.

I showed her the pregnancy test.

Her face immediately grew redder than I'd ever seen it before. "What were you thinking?" she asked angrily.

"I—"

"What are you going to do now?"

"I—"

Before I could answer one question, she was hitting me with another one. They were flying at me like killer bees.

"I hope you know you're going to have to get a job, Ebony."

I had dropped my head by that point.

"Did you tell Darnell?" she asked.

That particular question was the only one I could answer. "Yes," I told her. "He knows. We're going to be cool."

"Ebony being *cool* with it isn't enough to take care of a baby. You need money, stability, and an education."

She then told me to tell her everything there was to know about Darnell. Finally for the first time, I decided to lay my cards on the table about him. I'd been lying to her up until that point about his age and other things. I realized it was time to stop lying. I admitted he was twenty-one and a high school dropout. From the look on her face, it was obvious I'd broken her heart. I felt terrible.

The redness in my mother's face dissipated. With a sigh she reached for me, pulled me close, and said lovingly, "We're going to get through this."

As she held me, I felt protected. The extremity of the moment subsided slightly. But just as it did, she let me go, headed for the door and said, "You're going to have to tell your father."

Those words sent chills down my spine. My father was no nonsense. I knew telling him wouldn't be as easy as telling my mother. First I had dropped out of school with only a ninth grade education. Now this? He was going to kill me.

I called my father that evening, attempting to sound super innocent. I made small talk, asking him how he was doing.

"I'm cool and the gang," he told me like he always did when I asked him that question. I chuckled.

"Dad, I need to talk to you," I remember saying in a more serious tone.

"About what, Mama Poo?"

That was the nickname he'd given me. Hearing it at that moment made me feel so ashamed because I knew he'd probably never see me as his little Mama Poo again after the news.

I just came out and told him, "Daddy, I'm pregnant."

"What!" he screamed into the phone.

My body tensed. My face grimaced.

"You too? First your sister and now you? Both my babies having babies when you're only babies yourselves!"

All I could do was sit there and listen while hoping he'd calm down and forgive me.

"Who's the father? Is it that damn knucklehead little boy yo' mama say you runnin' 'round with?"

"Yes," I answered in a low tone.

"Well I'm going to have a talk with his ass. You can believe that."

He yelled some more about Darnell then asked, "So what now? What are you going to do from here?"

"I'm going to keep it."

"Ebony, I thought you would have learned from your sister."

"I did. It wasn't like I planned this."

We talked a little longer. As we did, he calmed down thankfully, but told me he definitely wanted to talk to Darnell. Before getting off the phone, he told me he loved me and that I was still his little Mama Poo. Hearing those words warmed my heart. They let me know he still had my back.

After that day, my father kept his word. He and Darnell had a talk. I later asked them what was discussed. Neither would tell me what was said. They just said it was grown men's business and didn't concern me. Well, whatever was discussed, I was just grateful that everything worked out. The baby growing inside my stomach would make us all family forever.

* * *

As time passed, my life moved like a rollercoaster, filled with plenty of ups and downs. Even my pregnancy didn't shield me from those downs. As I was preparing to bring the life of someone I loved with all my heart *into* the world, I was on the verge of almost seeing someone I loved with all my heart brutally *exit* the world.

Eight months into my pregnancy, on New Year's Eve, my mother gave a party to bring in the new year. Family and friends were there enjoying each other's company. Music played while beer and liquor was being consumed. Everyone was having a good time. While everyone partied, laughed, and sang old school song after song, I chose to sit up under Darnell, proud to be carrying his child. Obviously since I was pregnant, I wasn't drinking. I was content with just watching everyone else enjoy themselves.

As the party went on, I noticed that my mother and Tracey, my Aunt Debbie's boyfriend, were off in a far area of the room laughing and talking. It seemed harmless to me. They looked like they were simply having a good time like everyone else. It didn't look that way to Joe though. To him, it looked like Tracey was

59

hitting on my mother and she liked it. Watching Joe's face, I intervened. "What's going on?" I asked him.

"Your mother thinks I'm stupid," he said angrily.

I could smell the alcohol on his breath.

"That nigga over there is trying to talk to her. The shit's disrespectful. I ain't havin' it."

"It's not like that," I told him hoping to keep the situation from going where I knew it could end up. "You know she wouldn't do that. You're jumping the gun."

Ignoring me, Joe headed across the room, barging his way through the crowd, walking directly up to my mother. "We need to talk." He said it loud enough that others took notice.

The two of them headed to the back bedroom. As they did, friends and family looked at me as if to ask, "What's going on?" I basically tried to brush it off like it wasn't anything serious. Deep inside, I knew better.

The arguing began moments after Joe and my mother shut the door to the room. Tracey was the first to hear it. "I hear arguing," he said. The music was lowered while he and I headed back to the room. When we got there, Joe stormed out, cursing and shouting at everyone as he headed through the house to the front door in a tantrum.

"Just let him go!" I told everyone, hoping he would just go on about his business.

Joe kept raging, so several men tussled with him a bit, eventually putting him out. As they did, I walked into the backroom to see how my mother was doing. Unexpectedly, I saw her lying flat on the bed, holding her chest as blood gushed from underneath her hands.

"He stabbed me," she said pitifully.

My knees weakened. I couldn't believe it. It was then that I saw the knife lying on the floor and realized she'd pulled it from her chest herself. Rushing to her, I noticed that her face was turning blue. Immediately I yelled for help and called 9-1-1.

The wait for the ambulance was one of the longest of my life. I cried my eyes out, worried that she wouldn't make it as her blood soaked my hand and clothes. I held her in my arms tightly not knowing if this would be the very last time I would get to hold her.

Once the ambulance arrived, and my mother was stable enough, they rushed her off to the hospital. Sitting in that waiting room was torture. I couldn't sit still. I couldn't stop shaking. I couldn't stop thinking about her.

Finally the doctor came out and told me that she was going to be okay. She had a collapsed lung and would need a breathing tube to help her breathe for the next couple of weeks. But she would make it.

Until this day, I don't know what I would've done with myself if my mother had died that night. She'd always been stronger than any other woman I'd come across. She'd always been my rock. I can't, and couldn't, picture my life minus her. Without my mother, I don't think I'd be here.

After several weeks, my mother came home. Her arrival coincided with the birth of my first child, Darnell Jr., and for the first time, I was finally getting a taste of the responsibilities I'd seen my mother accept. They weren't that easy to swallow. Yet, I vowed to handle it though.

Of course my lifestyle changed. I had to apply for welfare, which was all I knew at that time. Unfortunately, it had become a family legacy. I hadn't been pushed, or forced to get a job. Even Darnell didn't want me working. It was cool with me though, because I could be around Darnell twenty-four-seven. I always followed him closely, slept under him when I could, and held him tightly documenting his days in a book I kept.

Darnell was a great father. He was always stopping by and contributing when he could. He was proud of his son and was proud to be a father. I can still remember him picking his son up, holding him in his arms, and whispering to him, "I'm not going to let you grow up to be like your dad. You're going to be better than me."

The words always brought tears to my eyes. They, along with the bond he was building with his son, had me really wanting to make things official. I wanted to marry Darnell. I constantly told him I was ready, but he always told me he wasn't. He kept saying he needed to get himself together first. I wasn't sure what that meant. All I could do was keep hope and faith that he'd come around eventually. In the meantime, reality's darkness casted its shadow over me once again.

Darnell came over with the bad news that he'd gotten into some trouble and he'd possibly have to do prison time. He wouldn't tell me exactly why or what was going on. But, since I knew he was selling drugs, I figured it was probably drug related. During that time, more and more young, black males were beginning to get swept off the street for selling crack in Cleveland's surrounding areas.

"Ebony, I'm sorry," he would tell me with guilt and pain in his eyes. "I know my son needs a father. I promise I'll make this better."

Holding me in his arms, I can still remember him saying, "God, I hope I don't have to go away from you and Darnell Jr."

The weeks leading up to the court date were rough for us all. His lawyer said he was facing up to five years. The possibility of him being gone for that long scared me to death and broke my heart. I couldn't fathom being without him that long. Just five *minutes* without him bothered me. Five years would be unbearable.

I was also worried about raising our son on my own. I knew my mother would help out just like she'd been doing, and my grandmother could always be depended on. But, it just wouldn't be the same without Darnell. He was a big part of it all. His absence would always make me feel like something important was missing.

Eventually Darnell's final court date rolled around. Surprisingly, I didn't go. I'm not quite sure why. I guess I knew deep down that despite the crying, praying, and hoping, he wouldn't be coming home that day like he'd been during the preliminary hearings. And I knew I wouldn't be able to take seeing them put those cuffs on him, leading him away from me.

Sadly I was right.

Darnell was sentenced to five years in prison. The moment I got the news, my world crashed down around me. I'd never been filled with so much uncertainty. Even with my mother and family holding me down, without Darnell it wasn't the same. I was left to figure out life on my own.

❧ CHAPTER 6 ❧

AN ASSIGNED PURPOSE

Each of us has an assigned purpose! Some of us are
assigned to touch one person during our time here on
Earth, while others are assigned to touch thousands,
even millions! Each assignment is similar to a
fingerprint, specifically designed for the particular
individual. A person who finds purpose in life, finds
life in their purpose!

Ebony's Life Lesson #7

THE HIGH'S & THE LOW'S

When someone you love is ripped away from you
and sent to prison, it isn't an easy thing to adjust to.
Darnell was my world, and I honestly didn't know how I
would live without him. I cried my eyes out and went
through withdrawal. My heart, my body—everything—
ached for him. It was hard. Really hard. But, as I'd
learned, life went on.

Soon after Darnell went off to do his time, I landed
my very first job at JC Penney. Now making my own
money, I decided it was time to spread my wings, and
move out on my own. Well, it wasn't completely on my
own. Dee Dee, Darnell's cousin, Charmaine, and I
decided to pool our money and get a place. It was crazy
now that I look back on it. Each of us had one child, was
unmarried, and none of our children's fathers were
around.

We made the best of our situation, to say the least. It was chaotic at times, since there wasn't a blueprint available to guide us. Of course, issues would arise with three women living under one roof. We had our fights and arguments, but for the most part, we got along and enjoyed each other's company. We were young, so we often partied and hung out until the wee hours of the morning, drank, and smoked a lot. What else would you expect from a group of young girls who were out on their own, and experiencing the world for the very first time? Even our landlord took a liking to us. He nicknamed us The Golden Girls.

Things really began to change for me financially. My job enabled me to buy whatever I wanted. I purchased the latest clothes and sneakers, and whatever I needed for my son. I was able to get my hair and nails done on a regular basis, something that I loved to do. With my own place and money, I could finally be my own woman. I was finally the grown woman I'd dreamed of.

Finding my independence came at the expense of Darnell's trust. The new clothes, fresh hairdos, and manicured nails brought lots of attention from men. Missing Darnell, and thirsty for attention, I fell prey to the numerous men who vied for my time, and ultimately my body. I loved Darnell, but it was difficult to stay faithful knowing he would be gone for so long. And it was even more difficult as a young woman, experiencing this new sense of adulthood. I was overwhelmed.

I just couldn't adapt to having absolutely no sex at all for an entire five years, after I'd become accustomed to having someone wrap their arms around me every night. I gave it an honest try, but I simply wasn't that mature. For me, it was only about the sex with the other men. I still loved Darnell too much, and although I gave away my body, my heart stayed his. Still, the infidelity eventually riddled my relationship with him.

Around that time, I picked up a new sort of hustle, if you can call it that. When money got tight, I made the dudes I slept with come out of their pockets. Now, I'm not ashamed to call it what it is.

I sold my body.

Back then, at only nineteen, I was still too young to quite understand that I was playing myself. I didn't see my behavior as disrespecting myself, and the body God gave me. I just figured if a man was going to get the privilege of having sex with me, I deserved to get a bill paid here and there, or have a little money stuffed in my purse. It was a part of the culture I'd been exposed to and adapted to well.

No harm, no foul. Or, so I thought.

Sooner than expected, Darnell was released from prison. Time had flown by quickly. He was able to come home early on shock parole, which grants probation to defendants after only a short time in prison, with the expectation that they've been "shocked" into a noncriminal lifestyle. To say I was truly happy was a lie. Yes, I was happy that Darnell was finally home, and that he and Darnell Jr. could finally reestablish their relationship. But during our time apart, I had become a different Ebony. I was used to being on my own, and not answering to anyone. I liked my lifestyle. With Darnell home though, I knew all that would change.

Darnell moved back in with his mother, but stayed with our son and me occasionally. With him so close, my male friends had to be cut off, at least temporarily. It was only temporary because shortly after Darnell got home, he began cheating *again*. I just couldn't catch him in the act. He was always too slick with it, but I knew. A woman's intuition is never wrong, so I started doing me once again. I didn't expect that my vindictive ways would came back to bite me sooner than I expected.

I wound up pregnant again.

Unlike the first pregnancy, I wasn't sure who the baby belonged to this time. Since I was cheating, I had no clue. Of course I couldn't tell Darnell that, so selfishly I suggested an abortion. He knew neither of us was ready for a second child, so he agreed to it without knowing the true reasons behind my decision.

I knew I needed to get my life straight at that point. I knew I needed to fall back from certain things and certain people. I was living way too foul, but I didn't know how to change. Although my behaviors were self-destructive, I couldn't help being drawn to them. It all had just basically become a part of me, a part that I couldn't let go of or walk away from.

Despite our flaws, Darnell and I decided to really go hard at getting things right between us. He suggested that we get our own place. He truly felt we needed our own, and that it was time we matured. I just went along with his idea.

Darnell found a job and began working. While he did, he preferred that I stay home to be a full-time mom. Once again, I depended on welfare to supplement my income, and concentrated on making a nice home for us. I'll admit, I liked taking care of our home and family. It made me feel so wifey-like.

"I'm going to make you my wife," Darnell would tell me often. "I promise you one day it's going down."

My heart melted each time he said that to me. I loved to hear those words. They made me feel like I was on top of the world. I'd smile every time, because I knew without a shadow of a doubt that he loved and belonged to me, despite his faults. I felt like good times were ahead.

I was so wrong.

My good times in life were few and far between, and never lasted for too long. This particular stage in my life was no different. At twenty-two, I got pregnant again. I was sure it was Darnell's this time, but the pregnancy came at such a bad time. Darnell couldn't leave the streets alone. His affinity for that life once again placed him in a bad position, staring down the barrel of jail time. This time it was only three months. Nevertheless, it was time away from our son and me.

I was so angry when Darnell gave me the news. "This can't keep happening!" I yelled. "It has to stop, Darnell."

He promised me that he would stop hustling and that he would get his life together. But all of his promises would have to wait until he got out. He was sent back to the penitentiary very quickly. I loved Darnell, and wanted to stick by him, but this time proved to be much more difficult than the last.

Most men don't realize that when they go away to prison, it's not just them doing time. The people they love are forced to do that time with them. Their loved ones may not be behind the walls or in a cell, but they are imprisoned in their own way. Life changes for them.

The entire household is affected. Everyone feels the sting right along with the person who's locked up.

Without Darnell paying the bills, and me now three months pregnant, welfare couldn't keep things afloat. So, I had to move back in with my mother. Lord knows I didn't want to. I was used to my independence. But what choice did I have now? It had finally hit me that my choices in life had put me in a bind. Here I was, a young, single mother with two kids. I didn't like the way that picture looked at all, but I wasn't ready to give up on Darnell or what we were building before he got locked up. I still wanted to marry him.

"Don't you think it's time y'all got married?" my father would ask. "Don't you think it's time he made you his wife?"

My father was right. I was riding with Darnell for a second bid in the pen. I realized it was time he made me his wife. He had no choice in the matter, I convinced myself. Taking matters into my own hands, I rushed to Walgreens and used their little greeting card machine to make a card to propose to him.

"Are you crazy?" folks asked me. "The woman isn't supposed to propose to the man. The man is supposed to propose to the woman."

I wasn't trying to hear anything that would discourage me from doing this. I was going to follow my heart. I sent the letter to Darnell, and waited on pins and needles for his answer. He answered yes. I was so happy. Immediately after he agreed to marry me, I began prepping for our wedding. When he finally came home, we got married just like planned. Ironically, Brains was the best man at our wedding. Shortly thereafter, we had our second son, Darnez. But as usual, my happiness only came in spurts, and not without problems. How could one person endure so many rough times?

Darnez's birth came with complications. I ended up hemorrhaging in labor, and needed a blood transfusion. I almost died that day. That close brush with death was what really brought me eye to eye with God. I knew I needed a relationship with Him. I just didn't quite know how or where to start. I knew I needed to figure it out. Something in my spirit told me I would need Him. I yearned for a relationship where I could pray for my family, and He would hear my prayers. It seemed as if we were missing our blessings.

Things had to change.

My father was happy to hear my wishes. He had become closer to God over the years, and attended church regularly. He and I started going to church together, and soon Charmaine began going with us too. I shared my life's frustrations and eagerness for a better life with them both.

"You need to pray," my father constantly told me. "God has you."

I began to do exactly what my father told me. I began to pray and build a personal relationship with God. I placed my heart and soul into it, and became proud of what I was creating with Him. I even slowed down on my drinking and partying, and convinced Darnell to get baptized with me. It was beautiful. But sadly, as I was welcoming God into my universe, Darnell, the man I loved more than the air I breathed, was about to leave it.

There are certain days, times, and moments that occur in each our lives in which we make a decision, and it changes everything. Forever. And from that point on, for the rest of your life, you regret that decision. You're left wishing with all your heart that you had done something—anything—differently. Uselessly, you wish you would've gone left instead of right, or that you would've said yes instead of no. For me, December 15, 2000 is a day, time, and moment that I made one of those decisions.

I'll never forget that day. A year into our marriage, Darnell and I got into a disagreement. Since getting out of jail, he had kept his word to stay out of trouble. He had become a family man, rarely leaving the house. But on this particular day, he wanted to go out, and I didn't want him to. We went back and forth until I finally gave in. With tears in my eyes right now, God knows I wish I hadn't. I wish with everything in my being that I wouldn't have let him leave the house that night.

Darnell left to go out and enjoy himself with a friend. Hours passed without me hearing from him. Before long, two o'clock in the morning rolled around. I'd been pacing the floor. It wasn't like him to stay out that late, especially on a work night. My gut told me something was wrong. Maybe he had been arrested. Maybe he was hurt. Whatever it was, I knew it was something. My stomach just didn't feel right. I grew worried, and began to call around to see if anyone had heard from him. I couldn't get anyone to answer their phones. Finally, I called his friend's mother. She answered. I asked if she'd seen Darnell.

"Oh my," she said with a troubled tone. "You haven't heard, have you?"

"No, heard what?" I asked.

She paused for a moment.

I gripped the phone and listened intently.

"Baby," she finally said. "Darnell was in a car accident."

My heart plunged.

"He was dead on arrival to the hospital."

I grew weak, too weak to hold the phone. It fell from my hand. With the memory of him walking out of the door earlier still in my mind, and tears falling from my eyes, all I could do was scream and collapse to the floor. As I did, Darnell Jr. and my nephew sat on the steps with no clue as to what was going on.

Moments after hearing the news, I prayed. I prayed as hard as I could. I needed strength. I needed *more* than strength. I needed something indescribable to get me through the moment, especially when I looked into Darnell Jr.'s eyes and realized I had to tell him that he was never going to see his father again.

I couldn't even logically grasp what I'd heard. All I knew was that I had to get to that hospital. I had hope that he was still alive. There had to be some kind of mix-up. I dreaded calling Darnell's mother, but I did. I told her that Darnell had just been in an accident. It didn't take long for her to get off the phone with me, and make her way to pick me up. I cried the entire ride to the hospital, praying it wasn't true. I wept like never before.

I got to the hospital, and my worst fears were confirmed. He was really gone. I was still in disbelief. I couldn't understand why. My heart burned. What was I going to do without my other half? What were my children going to do without a father? We were just together hours ago and now we were no more! The weight of his death bore down on me, forcing me to the lowest point in my life. I never thought I would ever rise again.

Eventually gathering myself, I was escorted to a chilly, silent room where Darnell's body was lying. It killed me to see him that way. It killed me to know he was gone. At first, I wouldn't accept it. I expected him to say something. I expected his eyes to open. I expected him to say everything would be okay; anything to let me know the moment wasn't real. None of those things ever happened.

All of our good times and smiles bombarded my mind and heart. I thought about the moment we met. Every memory and thought brought tears to my eyes, knowing we'd never get another chance to experience the good or bad together again. Finally, knowing I had to let go, I slid my hand into his, and kissed him softly on his cold, lifeless lips; those full lips that I had always loved so much. Then I placed my lips to his ear, and whispered a promise.

"I'm going to raise our kids just the way you wanted, baby." I meant that with everything in me! I knew that my husband loved his boys, and he wanted the best for them. I was going to make sure that happened.

With one final kiss, I said good-bye to my husband and friend forever.

CHAPTER 7

ENDURING PAIN

Pain is not meant to weaken your character, it is meant to strengthen who you are. It's exercise for the soul! Although pain may not feel good to you at the time, it is slowly building a person who will be able to withstand adversity as it inevitably comes our way. If we never experience pain, we will never gain the resilience needed to make it through this battle called life!

Ebony's Life Lesson #8

A WIDOW TOO SOON

Losing Darnell was literally like losing a part of me. I felt absolutely incomplete, like I couldn't survive without him. Some days, I felt like it was difficult to breathe, as if I was suffocating. It was as if the life was being sucked out of me. I couldn't eat. Food wasn't important to me; my taste buds wanted nothing except Darnell. Food couldn't keep me alive; nothing could but my husband. I cried so much my eyes were always bloodshot and swollen.

I dreaded waking up each morning because I knew it would be another entire day without Darnell. I yearned for his presence so much that I began walking around the house and sleeping in his clothes just so I could smell him. I spent moments closing my eyes and imagining the sound of his voice. Out of habit, around the time he'd usually arrive home from work, I'd watch the front door, expecting him to walk through it. I needed and missed him just that much.

Darnell's death also affected my family. Both my brother and my father cried often. Before that, I had never seen either of them shed a tear. The two of them really liked Darnell, so it hurt them to lose him too. It hurt me to see them cry. They were the backbone of my family, and the only strength I had left. Now they were weak. It was then that I realized just how much Darnell had touched them.

Although I had my parents, I was completely lost at that moment. I felt like I had no guidance or even purpose. Darnell and I had been together since I was fourteen. My life had always revolved around him. His words had always been the gospel to me. Without him or his words blessing my days anymore, I had no idea how to function. I honestly didn't think I'd *ever* discover my purpose in life.

The funeral was hard for me. It was almost as difficult as experiencing as the actual loss. I couldn't even approach his casket. I just couldn't. I preferred to remember Darnell alive. I only wanted to remember his smile and laughter. Looking into that casket would darken those memories. It would hurt too badly. I wouldn't be able to take it.

My two children, my father, my mother, and I sat in the front row at the funeral, listening to the sermon. I can still remember the preacher saying a lot about coping after the death of a loved one, like he'd been through the experience himself. I didn't know if he had, but his words eased my heart somewhat, even though I couldn't stop crying. His words gave me a tiny morsel of strength.

But that morsel soon evaporated. It was like an out-of-body experience. I sat there dazed and in shock, watching everyone step up to the casket and cry, or remove their hat to pay respect to my husband. I felt as if at any minute, somebody was going to shake me and I would wake up. At least I wished that would happen. When they closed the casket, my youngest son, Darnez, began screaming with tears in his eyes, "Where are you going with my daddy? Bring my daddy back!"

At that moment, practically the entire church erupted in tears. It was like Darnez, through his pain, had solidified the fact that Darnell was really gone. This wasn't a dream or even a nightmare.

It was reality.

And there was no turning back.

I can't lie. I contemplated suicide seriously after Darnell's death. Even my love for Darnez and Darnell Jr. couldn't inspire me. I just couldn't find it in me to go on. All sorts of ways to kill myself crossed my mind. I considered taking sleeping pills. I thought about slitting my wrists. Even though it was selfish, my mind wasn't on making anyone else feel better but myself.

I felt like I was mostly on my own, even though Brains, Darnell's good friend, would come over to keep the kids and to console me. We had grown to be more like brother and sister, so he did what he could to help out. But ultimately, the attention and support dwindled with the passing of time. At that time, I was so down in the dumps that I didn't realize people simply had to go on with their lives. They had to move on. I tried to move on too, but it was too much of a struggle, although my babies' smiles helped me along the way. But even they made the journey difficult, unknowingly, because they looked so much like their father. On some days, the resemblance was a blessing; on other days, it was heartbreaking. Eventually though, the heartbreak finally became too much and I reached a sort of breaking point.

One morning, around four a.m., I couldn't sleep. The bed seemed too big and empty. The walls felt like they were closing in and the oxygen felt like it was being sucked out of the room. I couldn't take it. I had to get out and get some air, so I hopped into my car and just started driving with no destination in mind.

As the night sky hung over the car's roof, I passed street after street. The Isley Brothers' classic, "Make Me Say It Again Girl", came on. While the song played, I couldn't help but think of Darnell and how he used to sing it to me. I could picture his huge smile and him spinning around, dancing and grabbing my hands. I missed him so bad at that moment. I couldn't believe out of all songs, this one came on! Was it a sign or what?

Of course more memories followed. Before long, the tears came. No matter how many times I wiped them away, more replaced them. My vision just grew more and more blurry. That was it. I couldn't go on any longer without my husband.

I pulled onto the train tracks, placed the car in park, and leaned back into my seat. I'd had enough. As I waited for the train, I realized that suicide was my only outlet. I wasn't thinking about my kids or my family. All I could think about was me. For moments I sat in silence; nothing around me existed or mattered. I simply waited for the train to take me away. Finally, a car pulled up behind me and began frantically blowing its horn. I hadn't heard it pull up, or even noticed its headlights illuminating my car's interior. But more importantly, I hadn't noticed the lights of the approaching train. I sat there. But something inside me made me put the car in drive and pull off the tracks. I guess I wasn't as ready to die as I thought.

When I got home, I gave serious thought to my children and how valuable we were to each other. It finally dawned on me how selfish it would be of me to leave them. I also realized and remembered something else, my relationship with God.

Psalm 23:4: Although I walk through the valley of the shadow of death, I shall fear no evil, for you are with me; your rod and your staff, they comfort me.

That scripture was my favorite and stuck inside my head. At that moment, I began to see things clearer. My mind and thoughts didn't seem so clouded. My soul didn't seem so dark. My heart didn't seem so empty. Inner strength filled me. I wanted to live for my children. I wanted to live for me.

I began praying again. I began pulling closer to God, knowing he would provide strength if I just accepted it. I still felt ashamed that I had pulled away from Him. Slowly but surely, there seemed to be some clarity in my world again. It also occurred to me that living in misery wasn't what Darnell would've wanted for me. He would've wanted me to push on. He would've wanted me to find direction in my life and be the mother to our children like I'd promised.

Pulling closer to God gave me the ability to start getting out of the bed each morning. It gave me the strength to start at least making an attempt at smiling again. Surprisingly though, it also gave me the strength to do one other thing that I *never* thought I'd ever be able to do. Forgive.

Darnell's friend, the driver of the car that killed him, was the most hated person in existence to me. I despised him for what he'd done, especially when I discovered that he actually walked away from the accident after pulling Darnell's body out of the car and leaving him on the side of the road. He walked home and called 9-1-1, but still, I'd be lying if I said I didn't wish *he* would've been the one lying on the side of the road that night. Thankfully, he didn't show up to the funeral. There was no telling what I, or Darnell's other friends and family, would've done to him.

Still, walking with God means forgiving those who hurt us. So one day I called him over to the house. When he arrived, the pain and guilt of what he had done was more than obvious in his eyes and face. I could see his conscience had been tormenting him. He was hurting just like me and everyone else who loved Darnell.

With all my heart, I sincerely told him, "I forgive you." I knew that I had to. I knew Darnell would want me to, and most of all, I knew God, the ultimate forgiver, would want me to.

We hugged.

I have to admit, I was surprised at myself for being able to do that. But the surprise of that moment didn't compare to the surprise I felt when I soon discovered something else. I was pregnant again.

Before Darnell's death, I probably would've loved the idea of being pregnant with his third child. But instead, I greeted the thought of it with worry. Darnell had been the breadwinner. Without him, finances were super slim. My welfare check wasn't even putting a dent in the bills. Eventually, I had no choice but to move my two children and my unborn child right back in with my mom.

While living with my mom, and trying to figure out exactly how to put the puzzle pieces of my life back together, my daughter, Dariell, was born. With the births of my first two children, I had Darnell by my side. This time, I didn't. Sadly, because of his absence, I couldn't even look at Dariell when she was born. It just depressed me too badly.

"Ebony, it's Darnell's daughter," my mother told me, at my bedside. "You have to see her. This child is a blessing."

I just turned away and cried, letting my tears run down my face and soak the pillowcase. I couldn't face my baby. Without Darnell, it just hurt too badly. I couldn't bear it. A couple of hours later, my mother brought Dariell into my room again. I was still too scared to face my daughter, but after a while, my mother successfully convinced me. Finally holding my baby in my arms, although we were now face-to-face, my mind and heart was still filled with worry and fear. I had no idea how I was going to take care of all of us. The only thing that gave me hope was that she looked just like her father. Her looks reminded me that I was holding a piece of him.

After leaving the hospital, just as I feared, times were difficult. It didn't take long to go through Darnell's small insurance policy, and money was hard to come by. Things looked so hopeless. The combination of the financial strain and missing Darnell drove me into another relationship.

His name was Shawn. He was handsome, helpful, and caring. He also had some of the same personality traits as Darnell, which attracted me to him even more. I really liked him, and our relationship grew quickly. As expected, several people, including my mother, felt I was dating too soon. They said I hadn't allowed myself to heal, and I was mistaking loneliness for love. Maybe they were right. But I'd never lost a spouse before, and I didn't know what to do, or how to handle it. I had no idea how long I was supposed to wait before starting a new relationship. And I certainly didn't know how to distinguish real love from anything else. I guess I was vulnerable.

Being with Shawn definitely began to make me happy. I loved being in his arms. I loved his attention. I loved his touch. It just felt so good to be in the comfort of a man again.

"You're trippin'," Charmaine constantly told me. "You're moving too fast. Do you know what you're getting yourself into?"

Despite her disagreeing with my new relationship, I moved forward with it. As long as it was making me happy, I felt it was no one else's concern. However, as my newfound happiness was brightening my life, one of Charmaine's decisions was about to darken hers.

I would always watch Charmaine's eleven-month-old baby, Daezel, whenever she went out to enjoy herself. While with Shawn, I was a homebody so watching my nephew wasn't a problem for me. One night though, I had plans, so I couldn't keep him.

Charmaine found someone else. That decision would shatter her world in the worst way a mother could imagine.

Daezel woke up the next morning crying and screaming. The people Charmaine had left him with had been drinking too much the night before. They were hung over and in too deep of a sleep to hear him. As they slept, their five-year-old daughter, who had cerebral palsy and a habit of washing her dolls in the bathtub, heard Daezel's screams. She went into his room to get him. She thought Daezel was a doll, and not knowing any better, she placed him in the tub. Unbeknownst to everyone, Daezel was drowning. By the time the adults awoke, got to him, and rushed him to the hospital, it was too late. He was pronounced brain dead.

My sister was completely distraught. But to make matters worse, she was charged criminally right along with Bianca, the girl's mother. It was her worst nightmare. I had a mountain's weight of regret on my shoulders and my heart. Just like letting Darnell walk out that door the day he died, I wished I could've gone back and changed my decision to watch Daezel when Charmaine asked me. That regret weighed so heavily on me. I knew if I had watched him that night, he'd still be here.

Suffering from loss and grief, Charmaine became a mirror image of me when I lost Darnell. The pain and regret was killing her like a cancer. It got to the point when it was obvious that she was contemplating suicide. Recognizing her state of mind, I refused to let her out of my sight. We stayed by her every moment of the day.

I constantly asked God for answers. I wanted to know why. Why was tragedy hitting my family so hard? I prayed on my knees for an answer. But rather than answers to my questions, life gave me something else instead—more tragedy.

ભ CHAPTER 8 ઇ

BATTLING GRIEF

*Pain will not go away until you face it! Pray for a
purpose from your pain because there is a reason,
a lesson, and a purpose behind that pain. Stop
asking God, 'Why me?' and start asking, 'Why
NOT me?'*

Ebony's Life Lesson #9

WARNING SIGNS

Losing my nephew only compounded my existing,
unresolved pain. Even though I truly hadn't gotten over
the loss of Darnell, it deeply bothered me that my
nephew never got a chance to live his life. It was unfair,
and I couldn't understand it, nor could my sister. I
couldn't protect my sister, my best friend. I couldn't
make things better for her like I used to up until that
point. It pained my heart to see her go through losing a
child. Yes, I had lost a husband, but not a child. We were
two lost souls!

The grief rocked our entire family. Without Daezel,
we all felt empty. We all felt like there was a hole in our
family that nothing, or no one, would ever be able to fill.
It was crushing, but sadly, it was only a preview of the
tragedy that was to come. I certainly wasn't prepared for
the next wave of heartbreak.

Now looking back on my life, I can recall something that I think is relative not only to my life, but the lives of everyone walking the earth. During a stand-up performance, the comedian Chris Rock said something that sticks with me these days. He said that when we meet new people and venture into relationships with them, we're not actually meeting the real person. In all actuality, whom we really are meeting is their *representative*, the person they choose to show us. We don't meet the *real* person until sometime later on. Sadly though, often times, the real person can be detrimental to your life.

Just like he'd helped me through the pain of losing Darnell, Shawn consoled me through the loss of my nephew. He really was my rock. He was my knight in shining armor. He could do no wrong in my book. What I felt for him was love. And that love grew and became stronger when shortly after my nephew's death, I found out some bittersweet news.

I was pregnant.

Yes. Pregnant…with Shawn's baby.

Scared and embarrassed about what others would think, I wasn't sure how to tell everyone. Sure, I loved Shawn, but I knew I'd become pregnant too soon. I had no one to blame but myself. I had done nothing to prevent it. Immediately after discovering the pregnancy, and telling my mother, she reiterated that Shawn and I were moving way too fast. She'd been saying it from the beginning and hadn't eased up.

In hindsight though, I think what was really going on was she'd seen something in Shawn that I couldn't see, something that really had her feeling that I needed to fall back. Later on though, those things she saw began to reveal themselves to me.

It all started with phone calls from multiple females claiming to be Shawn's exes. They all claimed he was a woman beater. During one call, two girls even called me on the three-way. I had no idea how they'd gotten my number, but thought it was very childish. Immediately, they repeated what had already had been told to me before.

"What, you think you special?" they asked me. "You think he's not going to do it to you?"

I shrugged off their words and told them not to call me anymore. I just thought they were jealous. Shawn was a good guy, so I just figured they still wanted him, and would be willing to do all kinds of catty mess to break us up. Little did I know, their words were warnings and prophecies of things to come, based on their personal experiences with him.

I should've listened. If several reputable people are saying the exact same thing about one person, it's the truth. There's no doubt about it. These days, I'd take those warnings and run for the hills, but I was young and naïve back then. As I said, when you first meet someone, they only reveal the side of themselves they want you to see. You don't meet the real person until later on. Well, Shawn was about to introduce me to the real him in a painful and unexpected way. But first, tragedy would deal my family yet another hurtful blow.

Charmaine was the first to notice our father's health problems. She'd moved in with him temporarily, and while there, she began to notice bloody tissues in the trashcan. She also noticed blood on his clothes. Worried, she asked him what was going on. He told her that lately he'd been coughing up blood, and didn't know why. Immediately, she told him he should go to the hospital. He chose not to go.

A couple of weeks later, the bloody coughs persisted, and he woke up one night having difficulty breathing. After getting to the hospital, multiple tests revealed that my father had something on his lungs causing the health issues. The doctors wanted to run more tests.

"Dad, stay in the hospital," we urged him.

Just being plain stubborn, my father refused to stay. He checked himself out. Worried about him, Charmaine called our aunts, his sisters, and told them what was going on, hoping they could talk some sense into him. It didn't work. Although he agreed to go back, he said he wasn't going until he was ready.

My father was the type of man who always had to run the show. He always had to have the last word. And in every situation he faced, it was always either *his* way or the highway. This situation was no different.

Terribly worried about his health, we stayed on him. We kept pressing and pressing him. We couldn't lose our father. We had to make sure he received the best medical attention possible. This time, we felt as if we actually had a chance to prevent anything from happening to our loved one, and we were willing to do whatever we could. Finally, he gave in and decided to check himself back into the hospital, but it came with a stipulation. He wanted to watch the Mike Tyson vs. Evander Holyfield fight with his kids and family. Once he'd watched it, he would let me drive him to the hospital. I agreed. After all, it wasn't too much to ask. Besides, I enjoyed watching sports with my father.

On the hot, summer night of the fight, we gathered at my grandmother's house. She didn't have air conditioning, so Charmaine, my brother Latroy, my Aunt Diane, several other family members, and I were all out on the porch watching the fight. My father was super excited, yelling and cheering as Tyson laid punches. Like always, he drank his beer while enjoying the moment.

When the fight was over, Shawn and I took my father to the hospital just like we agreed. As we drove, he told me how much he hated hospitals. I told him he was going to have to get used to them for the time being. After arriving at the hospital and checking him in, I kissed him, made sure he was okay, and finally left. I visited my father nearly every day after that night. I kept him in good spirits, and listened to him complain about wanting to go home. Soon after, the results of his latest tests came back.

My father had lung and throat cancer.

The news was devastating to all of us. We also discovered that he had a tumor blocking his airway. An operation was needed immediately to remove the tumor. Luckily, he agreed to the operation. And after having it, even with a tracheostomy tube inserted into his throat to help him breathe, his health began to improve.

On Father's Day, Charmaine, Latroy, and I went to visit my father. We took cards and balloons up to his room. He was so excited to see us all together and he smiled from ear to ear! He was fresh out of surgery and had just received the trach. He tried to talk, but couldn't. He began writing things down in order to communicate

with us. It saddened me to see him with the breathing
tube, and I guess it showed on my face. When it was
time for us to leave, my father called me to his bedside.
He had written something down for me.

*Don't be scared Eb. I'm gone be here to see this grandchild
born, and I'll be at the hospital just like I was for my other
grandchildren.*

He reached over and rubbed my stomach. After
reading it out loud, I kissed him, loving the sense of
calmness that came over me.

Next, my father gestured for my brother to come
over. Their note was private. Naturally I wanted to know
what it said, so after we left the hospital, I made sure to
ask.

"Eb, he told me don't tell y'all," Latroy said. "But he
told me to take care of my sisters."

I wasn't sure if he knew something I didn't, or if my
father wanted us covered until he came home from the
hospital. Whatever the case, it made tears roll down my
face, and my brother assured me that my father would be
okay.

Shortly after the operation, my father seemed to be
doing great, so we were completely caught off guard by
what happened next. My Aunt Patsy was at the hospital
visiting my father. She said the two of them were playing
cards and enjoying themselves. Everything seemed okay.
As they were playing, the nurse came in to clean his
trach. While they were cleaning it, my aunt stood by and
watched. Everything seemed to be normal. Moments
later, blood began spurting from my father's neck. My
aunt was immediately whisked out of the room.

Coming in from running errands, I checked my answering service and heard a message from Shawn. He told me to call him immediately. It was about my father. When I called, he told me I needed to get to the hospital as soon as possible. Snatching my purse, I dashed out, hopped in my car, and got to the hospital as fast as I could. I prayed to God for the best.

I'd prayed that prayer so many times before, and it was way too familiar. There I was again, riding to the hospital and praying to God. I asked Him to not let death take my father, and to send His angels to protect him. It was the same prayer I'd said for my husband.

But when I got there, it was too late. My family was sitting outside, with their faces swollen from crying. I knew without asking that my father was dead. My heart dropped. The one day that I didn't go see him, he'd died. I felt so bad inside and this would soon be added to my list of regrets.

Not now God, I thought to myself, as I felt my legs wobble. My father was never coming home. My family and I were crushed by the loss. We just stood in front of the hospital crying. We hadn't quite finished grieving over Daezel. That wound hadn't healed, nor had we recovered from the loss of Darnell. Now here we were facing another devastating loss. It was overwhelming.

We collected ourselves as best we could, and into the lobby. A moment later, we were approached by a hospital representative, which seemed weird to me because during the previous deaths I'd experienced, that had never happened. I was too hurt and destroyed at the moment to dwell on it. She told us she was sorry for our loss. She then escorted us onto an elevator and into a room where my father was lying.

My father looked so peaceful. He didn't look like he was dead. He looked more like he was resting. I was expecting him to open his eyes. I knew he was no longer in pain and I knew, for a fact, that he had gone on to meet the One that he'd spoken so highly of, the One he'd told me to always look to and to have faith in, and the One who loves unconditionally. God. That alone eased my pain and caused my tears to stop flowing.

My family strongly believed in God and knew it was time to pray. Brokenhearted, we joined hands around my father's deathbed and prayed for his safe journey to the other side. It was by far one of the most heartbreaking prayers I've ever spoken or been a part of, because it signified the end of what seemed like an era. The man who'd given me life was gone forever.

After the prayer, another hospital representative came in and asked if we wanted an autopsy performed. I didn't want one because I knew what an autopsy would make my father look like. I'd seen how terribly it had made Darnell and my nephew look. I didn't want to repeat that process with my father. He looked so peaceful and I preferred that he remained that way.

Ultimately though, the final decision was made by my aunts. They also didn't want an autopsy, so there wasn't one. Looking back shortly after, we all regretted the decision because after discovering the circumstances around his death, we all felt, and still feel, he died because his trach was improperly cleaned.

After my father's death, my bond with God helped me through, but it also pained me. I just couldn't

understand why He was doing this to my family. I
couldn't stop questioning why He was inflicting so much
pain on one family, over and over again with anguish. It
just didn't seem fair. I began to ask why my family was
being ripped away from me by death? Why was the very
God that I'd been taught to put all my faith and trust in
making me question His actions? My father had taught
me to never question God. Yet, I bombarded Him with
whys.

With no answers to my questions, I attended my
father's funeral with my mother, my children,
Charmaine, India, and Shawn sitting beside me. It was
difficult to make it through. My father had been the one
to hold my family up after Darnell and Daezel died, and
now, he wasn't here. The realization made our hearts
something far beyond broken, especially as we listened
to Shawn's mother stand in front of the casket and sing
to the church. Her voice, although beautiful, was bone
chilling. I'll never forget it.

After the funeral, I grew closer to Shawn. I needed
him. I guess I needed the guidance of a man, just like I'd
needed it from Darnell and my father. He showered me
with comfort, love, and wisdom. His love definitely
helped me find my way. Several months after the funeral,
I gave birth to our son and my fourth child, Shawn Jr.
Giving birth to him was a needed blessing. There had
been so much turmoil, grief, and unhappiness. I figured
my turnaround had come.

While unknowingly pregnant with my daughter, I'd
lost my husband, and during this pregnancy, I'd lost my
nephew and my father. My father didn't keep his
promise to be here for the birth of his grandchild, and I

was hurt. Yet, I knew my father would want me to celebrate the gift that God had given me, so I embraced Shawn Jr. with open arms and tears of joy. The new life was like a breath of fresh air to my family. It felt good to us, if only for a moment, to be able to celebrate the arrival of life instead of the death of a loved one.

Also, although several family members, including my mother, had disagreed with my relationship with Shawn, they were now warming up to him after witnessing how much he seemed to love me and the kids. That meant a lot to me. I had always wanted them to accept him the same way they'd accepted Darnell. I wanted them to see the same attributes I saw in him. Now that they did, it felt great to me. Sadly though, it wouldn't feel great for too long.

From what I've discovered about domestic abuse, the abuser more often than not, appears to be a great guy in the beginning of the relationship. His charm is something that a woman usually welcomes, so she's usually swept off their feet. He's caring and honest, so we believe in him and the candy-coated words that he speaks. Then out of nowhere, like Jekyll & Hyde, that façade disappears. He becomes the type of man that she's only heard about, or seen on TV or in the movies. This type of man was now my reality, just like so many other women all over the world.

One day while Shawn and I were driving around the city, an attractive female strutted by. Shawn nearly broke his neck to get a better view. Obviously, I felt disrespected.

"Well, damn. If you like her that much, you might as well get out of the car and walk with her."

94

"You trippin'," he replied, shrugging it off and dismissing me.

"I am not trippin'. That was so disrespectful."

Suddenly, he got angry. *Extremely* angry. His face twisted into an expression I'd never seen. He didn't look like *my* Shawn anymore. He looked like a stranger. Catching me completely off guard, he took the palm of his hand and pushed my face away from him. I didn't know how to register what he'd done at first. I was completely shocked. He'd never put his hands on me before.

As we drove on, I thought back to what those girls had told me about Shawn being violent. But I quickly dismissed those thoughts. I gave him the benefit of the doubt. I began to tell myself that maybe I deserved it. Maybe I said something I shouldn't have. It had to be my fault. I'd pushed such a sweet man to put his hands on me.

I thought about the kids. I thought about how accepting my family had become of Shawn. Everyone liked him now. All of those thoughts made me let what he'd just done fall by the waste side. Besides, it wasn't like he'd actually *hit* me. It was just a shove. Little did I know, shoves eventually become punches, kicks, and beat downs.

Shawn was about to give me a crash course in all of it.

Chapter 9

Love Is A Drug

The love that we have for another human being can be more addictive than any other drug. We may search for that adrenaline rush that love provides, and begin to look for love in all the wrong places. What we need to realize is that God can only give real love. Wait on your perfect love from God!

Ebony's Life Lesson #10

LOVE IS BLIND

Life is like a road. Sometimes it lies straight ahead; sometimes it twists, turns, and curves. No matter what direction it takes, you never know what lies ahead or where it will lead. You don't know what sort of hand it will deal you. You just know that you have to travel it, no matter what.

I never imagined that my relationship with Shawn would head in such a traumatic direction. But I would soon learn another valuable life lesson. Hurt people hurt people.

Many would say I should've walked away from the relationship at the first sign of trouble. But, it's very easy to judge a person and say what they *should* or *shouldn't* do in a situation, especially without actually walking in their shoes. We all have our opinions about other people's situations and relationships. However, when you love someone, walking away from them is much easier said than done.

How many times have you stuck it out or *tried* to stick it out with someone because you loved them, whether it be a friend, child, boyfriend, or loved one, despite the fact they may have hurt you? How many times did you allow them to break your heart when you knew you shouldn't have? How many times did you allow them to cross a line? We've all done it. Our circumstances may be different, but we've all been through it one way or the other.

Love is like an addiction. You want it and you crave it. It can make a fool of us. It can make us all look stupid at times. Love grips us so hard, and sometimes, we just can't break free. I guess that's why I chose to enter this particular dark stage of my life, and remain there for two years.

From the moment Shawn pushed my face in that car, the next two years gradually became pure hell for me. Every day, our relationship moved further and further away from the happy-go-lucky couple we once were. He was no longer the caring person I had grown to love. He became a monster, a violent stranger I didn't know. Before that, I had no idea someone I actually loved with all my heart could be so eager to hurt me. I would've never expected it.

I erased the first violent incident from my mind. Since I loved him, I didn't consider it an actual *hit*. Since it didn't seem like a concrete act of violence, I overlooked it and didn't think anything similar would happen again. Many women in this type of situation choose to focus only on the good in the man, and to deny the reality. I was no different.

Most of the times with Shawn were good. When we got along, we were great. But things didn't always stay that way. We had arguments like any other normal couple. Usually, we'd either end our nights with great sex or a terrible fight. There was no in between. It was either really good or really bad.

Shawn and I decided to move in together. Soon thereafter, the second violent incident occurred. It's funny, I'd sworn to my sworn to my sister that I would never be in a situation like this. And here I was.

Shawn and I were sitting around one night, enjoying ourselves and having a few cocktails like we'd often do. While drinking, we typically enjoyed each other's company. The night started off sweet, and quickly turned sour when we began to argue. The argument was so insignificant and trivial—so petty—that I still can't remember what caused it. What I do remember is that in the midst of the argument, Shawn smacked me so hard that I saw all types of bright colors and lights. My knees buckled. My entire body trembled.

I hadn't expected the slap. It was only the second time he'd placed his hands on me, so I didn't see it coming. It was at that point that I realized he had a very short fuse, especially when it came to a woman mouthing off to him. As I sat there, stunned, upset, and enraged, I lunged for him. I had to fight back and defend myself; I wanted to hurt him too. We tussled and fought.

Afterwards, Shawn felt bad for what he'd done. I did too. Even though he was a man, I got some good shots in. Shawn felt the need to make up with sex, and as I would soon find out, our makeup sex was the best. It was as if he was apologizing with every stroke he made. I loved it, and always fell right back into the trap! I was caught up in what I thought was love. After all, he told me he was sorry, right? At the time, I was so gullible that I believed his words. I know now what I really feared—being alone. I had already gone through hell and back with the loss of Darnell, and raising three grieving children. My life was nothing that I would wish on my worst enemy.

I gullibly listened as Shawn told me he was sorry, and that he would never do it again. To be honest, I believed his words. I believed in my heart that the slap was just an isolated incident, but the distressing thought of loneliness tugged at my heart. That wasn't something I wanted to venture back into, and it played a part in me taking Shawn back again and again. I guess I saw the slap as just a tiny sacrifice necessary for happiness.

The relationship went on without me looking back, believing he would never hit me again. Eventually though, he did. I wanted to believe that Shawn would change and that this was just another isolated situation, but it wasn't, as so many domestic violence incidents are not either.

This time, I was standing in the living room of our house when Shawn came in from doing club promotions. He'd removed the car's radio from the console, and had it in his hand. Out of nowhere, and for no reason, he threw the radio as hard as he could directly at my face. It hit me in the forehead and left me bleeding. With blood running down my face, I was frozen, unable to move. Did he really just hit me with a heavy, metal radio? I didn't want to believe what he'd just done was deliberate.

In an instant, Shawn was at my side, taking me in his arms. "Baby, I'm sorry. I didn't mean it. I swear I didn't. I was angry about something and took it out on you. I'm so sorry, Eb."

Luckily the gash was a small one that didn't require me to go to the hospital. Still, of course, I should've gotten out of the relationship. I should've called it quits. But just like when he'd slapped me, he said he was sorry; this time immediately. He then took me in the bedroom and made love to me. Sexing me had become the norm after his abuse. I guess along with gifts, that was his way for making up for his actions. I accepted it, and life went on.

As our relationship pressed forward, the many good times outweighed the bad. The days weren't always dark, and Shawn wasn't always menacing. He could be a sweetheart at times. He was always a good father to Darnell's children, as well as Shawn Jr. I can remember family outings and movie nights with all of us hugged up on the couch. We all loved and treasured those moments. Those were the moments when we most resembled a family.

Also, Shawn's occupation as a promoter afforded us trips to other cities, and even allowed me to meet a number of celebrities like Paul Wall, Juvenile, and 8Ball & MJG. During those times, I felt like his queen. I felt special. Those particular moments always reminded me of the Shawn he was before the abuse began; the Shawn I fell in love with, enjoyed, and would do anything for.

But eventually, the Shawn I hated would show up out of nowhere as if the old Shawn never even existed.

Even with the exciting lifestyle, the arguing didn't slow down at all. In fact, it increased, and I couldn't understand why. During our next big blowout, Shawn was drinking a bottle of beer. Suddenly, he stood up with rage in his eyes. The next thing I knew, he'd slung the bottle directly at my head. As he did, I blocked my head and face with my arm. Unfortunately for me, the bottle hit my forearm with so much force it shattered. The bottle must've cut a vein. It wouldn't stop bleeding. I ended up going to the hospital.

While getting stitches, the nurse asked me details about what happened. That's when the lies kicked in. I made up a story, saying I'd gotten into a fight at the bar. I'm not sure if she believed it or not. I do know the police were in my room moments later, also asking me what had happened.

In hindsight, I should've told the truth. I should've had Shawn prosecuted. He should've been stopped from putting his hands on me, and possibly any other woman. Yet, I remained silent. *His* abuse was *our* secret. I just couldn't tell the police what he'd done to me. I loved him, and the last thing I wanted to do was see him locked up. I couldn't do that to the man I was crazy about. Not the father of one of my children. Refusing to see that happen, I chose to tell the cops the same story I had told the nurse. They accepted my fabricated story, wrote out a report and left.

I walked out of the hospital that night hoping to place the incident behind me. I had no idea the violent episodes, up until that point, weren't even the tip of the iceberg. After some time went by, things didn't get any better. Our fights escalated. Then, the brutal beatings began. The level of physical abuse he inflicted on me couldn't compare to the previous slaps and pushes. Shawn had graduated to beating me to a point that I regularly had black eyes, swollen lips, and a busted nose. The abuse happened frequently, and for no reason at all. He'd just lose his temper and snap.

Even though I was never really a makeup kind of girl, I would wear concealer and foundation to cover my bruised eyes if I had to go out or do things with the children. But, for the most part, I would stay in the house until the bruises healed. I hated having to cake the makeup on my face to cover what he had done.

I never told my family about the abuse. I wanted to keep up the façade. I wanted to believe that Shawn was a good man, and I wanted them to too. The last thing I wanted people to know was that he, the children, and I weren't what we appeared to be. Having our secret discovered would be humiliating. Eventually though, I could no longer hide the abuse.

My mother was the first to notice the endless black eyes. She'd ask what happened, and I'd make up lies to protect Shawn. Soon, other family members also began to notice. I'd lie to them too, mainly because I knew the drama it would cause if they knew I was being beaten. To keep things calm, I preferred to keep it to myself and handle it on my own. The only way I knew how to handle it was to just keep taking the beatings.

Finally, Shawn realized things had to change. He said he loved me. He said he loved our child, and the very last thing he wanted to do was lose that. With that said, he was more than ready and willing to get himself together. I believed him. I could see the love in his eyes. I could hear the sincerity in his voice. At that moment, I really think he wanted to change. He realized he had a problem and that it needed to be fixed. He decided to try hard to control his anger. He was just a hurt man, who didn't know how to deal with his pain, so he hurt me; the case in most abusive relationships. Our relationship was broken. I had a past that allowed myself to be abused, and he had a past that allowed him to be the abuser. We both recognized this. We called a counselor, but never executed our plan. The intentions were there, yet we didn't move forward.

Big mistake.

Little did I know, all abusers, including the ones who admit their problem and say they'll change, have one thing in common.

They never do.

෬ **CHAPTER 10** ෨

GAINING COURAGE

Have the courage to stand up for what you believe in. You can't doubt yourself. Never ever force-feed yourself anyone else's beliefs! Doubt & courage are like oil and water; they'll never mix. Be courageous in all that you do!

Ebony's Life Lesson #11

MOVING ON

There are many things that fuel an abusive relationship. In my case, my love for Shawn, and hope for our future, convinced me to accept his abusive behavior. I always wanted to give him the benefit of the doubt, and I believed that he really would change. I had the utmost faith in him. I really, really believed that each slap, punch, or all out beating would be the last. I definitely thought that was the case when he finally admitted to having a problem, and promised me he would stop.

My thoughts couldn't have been more wrong.

Despite his promises, the beatings started up again. After one particular beating that left me with yet another black eye, I also caught him cheating on me. I was devastated. Then, I became frustrated. I thought about how I'd walked around with black eyes, while constantly lying to my friends, all in an attempt to keep up the act. I wanted people to think I had a good man, when in reality, he wasn't just beating me; he was also cheating on me.

The mental and physical abuse had to end.

I'd had enough that night. I decided to be the one to do the snapping.

Shawn walked in around two a.m., acting as if cheating on me wasn't a big deal. When I questioned him, he said he didn't want to talk about it. I wasn't having it though. I was pissed. So when he went to sleep, I grabbed the iron, headed into the bedroom, and hit him with it, knowing what the consequences would be. I didn't care. I was angry and I wanted to fight, win or lose.

Strangely, I had begun to exhibit the very abuse that I was enduring. Would that really solve the cheating issue? No, it wouldn't, but I decided to listen to the devil on my shoulder.

As expected, Shawn jumped out of the bed, grabbed me, and started beating me. This time though, unlike the others, I fought back hard. I kicked, punched, scratched, and did whatever else I could to gain some sort of advantage. I was trying to do extreme damage. I wanted him to suffer and feel the pain he'd so often inflicted on me. Ironically, Shawn fought me just as hard. He slung me around like a rag doll; all over the room, and against walls so hard that the entire house shook with each impact.

It was an absolute battle.

During past incidents, I'd only tried to fight back. This time, I was fighting back for real. I tried my hardest to lay on him everything he'd painfully inflicted on me.

106

Plus, I was fighting out of the frustration, anger, hurt, and betrayal brought on by his abuse. It was all just culminating inside me and needed to be unleashed. As I swung, I could see each moment he'd hit me playing inside my mind. I remembered every time he'd hurt me. Those visions drove every punch I threw. But despite how hard I fought, Shawn was stronger. He eventually got the best of me.

My vision blurred as Shawn punched me in the face so hard I thought he would break my jaw. My body ached as he pinned me to the floor and punched me in the ribs. I gasped heavily for air and clawed at his hands, digging my nails into them as he wrapped both of them around my throat and squeezed. It broke my heart as he did, and as I stared up at him from behind a veil of tears, I couldn't believe the man whom I thought loved me would do this.

Luckily, the kids were in a back room. They never came out, but I could hear them crying as we fought. I could hear them screaming. It made me think of that moment when Charmaine and I first saw Joe beat our mother so badly that she's miscarried. When it happened to her, I never would've dreamed or imagined it would one day happen to me.

When the fight concluded, I felt that our relationship did too. We made up like always, but it wasn't the same. There was a disconnection, and we both felt it inside. The love was still there, but the fact that we'd gone so hard at each other this time really created a shift. Things were coming to an end.

Shawn and I decided to live apart, but didn't officially end our relationship. Not wanting to move

back with my mom, I simply found another house.
Shawn moved back in with his mother. I had no
problem with it, although afterward, the two of us began
to grow distant. Our need to spend time together began
to splinter. Shawn threw himself into his work. He began
promoting more and more events, while also working
with a local rap group that he was trying his hardest to
get off the ground. I'm not sure if he was cheating at that
time. With him out of my eyesight, there wasn't an
ounce of trust.

Despite our distance, we still stayed in touch,
especially for the kids. But even the love for them
couldn't change Shawn's abusing ways. The latest burst
of violence put a fear in me that I'd never forget.

One day, I went to visit Shawn at his mother's.
While there, he and I got into yet *another* argument. It
was almost impossible for a day to go by without some
sort of negative, verbal discourse. This time though,
instead of hitting me, he did something I never *dreamed*
he would do.

He pulled a gun on me.

I was in absolute shock as Shawn aimed the gun. I
thought for sure he was going to shoot me. My heart
pounded inside my chest as I stepped back, keeping my
eyes on the gun. I was terrified it would go off. I wasn't
sure if he would use it to kill me. But I remembered the
look he had on his face when he'd nearly choked me to
death. He had a similar look on his face now. My life
passed in front of my eyes.

"What are you gonna do with that?" I was scared,
but I didn't think he had the courage to do it. "I love
you."

I meant those words. I really did love him. I always wanted nothing but the best for him, and I never had any problem showing and proving that to him. I showed it through action every day. I showed it by sticking with him despite the abuse. I showed it by being his biggest fan and urging him on as his promoting career moved ahead. Couldn't he see that?

Shawn eventually put the gun down and walked downstairs. Immediately I grabbed it. Strangely though, it never crossed my mind to kill him. No matter what he had done to me, I never wanted to see him hurt, let alone killed. I didn't even want him locked up. I just couldn't find it in myself to do any of those things to him even though he deserved it. It should've shamed him that he had no reservations about doing those things to me. I just wasn't built that way.

Still I went back to him. Shortly after that incident, during another argument, he got so angry that he twisted my arm until it snapped. I ended up in a sling. But just like the other times, I refused to tell the police and my family the truth. I was approaching my breaking point though.

Finally it came.

One of my cousins threw a party. Everyone was enjoying themselves, including me. Shawn though, had a little too much to drink. He instigated an argument with me in front of everyone, for no reason other than he was just too drunk. This time, unlike the others, he decided to be bold enough to try to abuse me in front of people, including my family.

Bad mistake.

My cousin stepped in to protect me. He and Shawn began fighting violently. Fists flew and punches were being thrown unmercifully in all directions. Shawn was no match though. My cousin beat him pretty badly. He inflicted the same beat down on Shawn that he had inflicted on me during numerous occasions. Obviously, he deserved it. I left the party, wanting no part of the drama. Embarrassed and with wounded pride, Shawn left also.

That night, when I got home, I went to sleep on my couch. Strangely sensing something or someone, I awoke to the darkness of my living room at about four or five o'clock in the morning. Immediately, with beams of moonlight shining across his face from the window, I saw Shawn standing over me, looking like a villain from a movie. I was beyond startled as I rose up quickly. My heart pounded through my chest. I felt helpless, and knew the moment wasn't going to be good. I had no idea how he'd gotten in. I hadn't given him a key. It was obvious that he'd broken in. And from the angry look on his face, it was also obvious that he'd come for trouble.

Shawn began screaming and yelling at me. I was every bitch and hoe in the book. He yanked me into a tight embrace. For several minutes, his heavy, heated breathing sent chills through my body. After struggling with him, I broke free and ran for the stairs as fast as I could. As I quickly made it up several of them, trying to take at least two at a time, he caught me and dragged me back down so hard I thought my spine was going to break. I could feel each staircase banging against my back as I was dragged down one by one. Once at the bottom, Shawn began beating me some more. I escaped from him again, and dashed to the bathroom, attempting to shut the door.

Before I could, he caught the door, and shoved it open so hard that I stumbled backwards. He pushed me, and I fell into the bathtub. On my way down, I grabbed hold of the shower curtain. The curtain, along with the rod, came crashing down on top of me. Shawn then grabbed the rod and began beating me with it relentlessly. He wouldn't let up, calling me names with each swing. I couldn't do anything to protect myself but curl into a ball and hope he wouldn't kill me. Each blow seemed to hurt worse than the last. I thought it would go on forever. And it honestly got to the point that I thought he was really going to kill me this time. I didn't doubt it at all.

Shawn finally grew tired and left the bathroom, leaving me bruised, battered, and bloody. This beating was the worst by far. The others paled heavily in comparison. I had two black eyes, bruises all over my back, imprints from the curtain rod all over my body, and my body ached something horrible. Along with the physical pain, the emotional pain was worse than ever before.

My heart hurt.

My soul hurt.

My spirit hurt.

My pride hurt.

Everything inside me was in shambles. I finally had enough.

I loved Shawn; maybe more than I should have. I still love him until this day. Until this particular beating though, I'd made the mistake of loving him more than I loved myself.

I didn't realize the importance of self-love. If I had just loved myself a little more, I would've put a stop to the abuse when it first began. Allowing Shawn to violate me could not continue. I finally realized that night that I deserved better. I no longer wanted to lie for him. I no longer wanted to protect him; after all, he hadn't kept his promise to my father to protect me. His abuse would never end. With that realization, I did what I should've done a long time ago. I ended the relationship for good. Shawn moved to Texas with another woman, and that was it.

We were done.

⌀ **CHAPTER 11** ℔

A BETTER FUTURE

You have to let go of the wrong that has been done to you in order to grasp all that is within you! Letting go of the evil that's been done to you gives the good in you a chance to live! Change will only come once you've realized that the decisions you have previously made have gotten you in your present situation. Decide that you want a better future!

Ebony's Life Lesson #12

LETTING GO

One of the strange things about breakups is that, at least for a while, you can never really leave them behind. You bring baggage from old relationships with you into the new ones. Sometimes, the baggage hinders you from having a successful new relationship. Other times, it can be absolutely necessary to keep you on your toes. It protects you. That baggage can help you to not make the same mistakes again.

Finding true love after Shawn proved to be difficult. His abuse meant that I was constantly on high alert with every man I met. In every relationship I ventured into, I looked for red flags: cheating, bad tempers, controlling tendencies, speaking to me rudely—any behavior that I considered to be disrespectful. If a man asked to check my phone or questioned my whereabouts, I was turned off.

Whenever a new man in my life began exhibiting those traits, I cut him loose, immediately. It was nothing personal. Some probably would've turned out to be genuinely good men, but I couldn't take the chance. Shawn had taken me through hell and high water. He'd left me too wounded and scarred. He'd hurt me in almost every single way a man could hurt a woman. I wasn't going to take any chance whatsoever on that happening again.

Also, while exploring new relationships, it became customary to hold my feelings back. I wouldn't allow myself to fall in love or get really caught up in a man. I felt that love and emotions could cloud a person's judgment. They got in the way, convincing you to give people the benefit of the doubt when you shouldn't. Emotions closed your eyes to red flags, and your ears to a person's lies. I refused to let that happen ever again.

My experience with Shawn also piqued my interest and desire in publically speaking about domestic violence. I knew there were plenty of women going through what I'd gone through, and that my story would possibly help them. I hoped that my story could even help women to avoid abusive relationships and situations all together.

I spent the two years following my breakup with Shawn doing a lot of soul-searching and reflecting, which I really needed. I focused on my kids, stayed out of serious relationships, and worked on becoming a better, stronger me. Being on my own gave me a peace of mind that I never quite had before. This was my transformation. Ironically, my mother went through a transformation of her own. She'd gotten the courage to leave Joe. That sent a message to me, loud and clear.

I looked back on my past mistakes, as well as my mother's mistakes. I realized hindsight was definitely 20/20. At that moment, I saw the bad choices and wrong turns that I hadn't seen before. I remembered advice that I received, but disregarded. Everything became so clear. I realized I had to make some changes, starting with returning to school to get my GED.

I seemed to have finally found peace and direction in my life. But no significant portion of my life, no matter how peaceful, is complete without at least a touch of madness. Well, this particular touch of madness was about to turn my relationships with certain family members and friends completely upside down.

I need you to understand something. The heart can't help who it loves. It can't help who it falls for. The heart has a mind of its own. With that said, I'm not saying what I did was wrong or right. I'm just saying that I followed my heart.

Around this time, Brains resurfaced again. We'd lost touch during my relationship with Shawn. As my children's godfather, he never stayed away too long and was always willing to help me with the kids. We'd become close, but never crossed any lines. We were strictly friends.

Brains, who I called Shannon, had always been a genuine person. He never allowed his success to change him. He was also like Darnell in many ways. I guess that's why the two of them were such close friends and why I treasured his friendship. Since they were so much alike, and had been so close, having Shannon as a friend felt like having a part of Darnell with me. Shannon had swag. He was super handsome and knew exactly how to treat a lady. I'd always noticed those things about him.

I ran into Shannon at a bar one night while out with family and friends. We hadn't seen each other in years, so it was great to see him. We talked a bit, remembering the good times. Eventually we had a couple of drinks together, continuing our walk down memory lane until my friends were ready to go. I wasn't, so Shannon told me that he'd take me home.

During the ride from the bar later that night, we decided that we didn't want to end our reunion so soon. We hadn't seen each other in so long, and a few hours together just didn't feel like long enough. We decided to go to his house and continue kicking it there.

Before long, we were at his place, talking, laughing, and joking around like we'd always done. Then, out of the blue, our eyes locked and we kissed. Kissing led us to the bedroom, and soon to sex. We had sex all night long, only to wake up staring at each other, trying to figure out what just happened? What had we done? More importantly, now what? We were both embarrassed and ashamed. Yet, it was something so magical that we wanted to do it again and again.

Neither of us ever intended for our relationship to go beyond friendship. But sometimes life's intentions and ours aren't on the same page.

Shannon and I began to develop real feelings for each other. We hid it for quite some time, lying constantly along the way. We'd tell my sister and kids that I was dating Shannon's roommate, and that he was coming to pick me up for his friend. But those lies didn't fly for long. Soon it was time to come clean.

We exposed the truth, and the children and I moved in with Shannon to start our new family.

Looking back, maybe it was wrong. Maybe because of who he was to Darnell, I should've ended the relationship when I started falling for him. I honestly don't know. All I know is that it felt right. He made me happy. Once word got out about the two of us being together, all hell broke loose. Darnell's family was pissed. Scathing insults and opinions were thrown at us from every direction.

"He's your children's godfather," One family member said.

"You should be ashamed of yourself."

"Darnell is turning over in his grave right now," my mother added.

"Hoe."

"Tramp."

"Slut."

As they spat venom, I couldn't really see anything wrong with what I had done. My feelings for Shannon had grown even stronger. He was sweet, and treated me with respect. He was always giving me positive advice, and motivating me. Since we started out as friends, we also had a lot in common. We could talk about things from our pasts that we couldn't talk about with other people.

Our closeness also allowed me to spill my heart to him about what I had gone through with Shawn and also about the rape. After telling my story, I also told Shannon about my idea to start a blog to share my story with abused women and teens who lost their way. He pushed me to make it a reality. He was always doing things like that. He was always telling me the only thing that held me back was me, and that I could do absolutely *anything* I put my mind to. No man had ever instilled that in my head before. Still, no matter how happy Shannon made me, not everyone agreed with the relationship.

My mother was absolutely against us being together. Charmaine was too. Shannon's ex-girlfriend didn't like it either. Darnell's brother was so pissed off about our relationship that he threatened to kill us. It was definitely a messy situation. But Shannon and I really loved each other. If others couldn't accept it, oh well.

With Shannon pushing me towards my goal, I started a blog. In it, I laid out the naked truth about my relationship with Shawn, bearing my soul for the entire world to see. I didn't hide anything. I gave them every detail, and relived every moment. I shared my pain and my sadness. I wanted everyone who read it, especially those going through the pain of domestic violence, to know there was a light at the end of the tunnel. I wanted them to know they could be survivors too.

After publishing the blog, I felt a sense of relief. I felt like a huge weight had been lifted from my shoulders. It felt good. But it didn't last too long. After reading what I'd written, and realizing that I truly had exposed *all* my secrets about my domestic abuse, it scared me. I began to wonder if people would really see me as a survivor, or as a dumb woman who stayed in an abusive situation long after she should've left. I began to feel embarrassed about my abuse. I began to second-guess myself. My feelings overwhelmed me so much that

I deleted the blog after just two days. When I told Shannon what I'd done, he urged me to reconsider. I couldn't do it. Not until I knew I was ready.

Along with creating my blog, Shannon also encouraged me to try my hand as an entrepreneur. He had plans to start several businesses, and he wanted me to be involved with them. He talked me into enrolling in an online school to take some Business Administration classes. I was discovering new things about myself every day with him. Most importantly, I was learning to empower myself.

He also taught me that the ultimate strength came from my relationship with God. No previous boyfriend, not even Darnell, had taught me that. And although I'd already developed my relationship with God, it felt so good to finally have a man in my life who shared that same philosophy. Honestly, it was during this time that I realized that I'd spiritually and emotionally died many times before; the molestation, the rape, the domestic violence, and the constant struggles had all shaped who I'd become. Deep inside, my heart assured me that good times were on the way.

In 2010, Shannon and I began attending The Word Church, along with my children. The experience was mind-blowing compared to my experiences at other churches. The pastor was young and relatable. He wasn't afraid to talk about his humble beginnings, or things he'd experienced in life. He was able to preach about real life situations. The congregation could definitely relate to most of his sermons since we had either been through it, or were going through it as he spoke. Ironically, it seemed that nearly every sermon ran parallel to my day-to-day life. I could be going through something during the week, and when I would go to church that Sunday, the young pastor's sermon would mention exactly what I had been through. It was like he was speaking directly to me.

To make church more appealing to all types of people, The Word Church allowed churchgoers to dress however they wanted. We could come in Timberland boots, jeans, sneakers, or whatever. Obviously at other churches, although they preached all were welcome, they'd give you a side eye if you showed up dressed like that. I loved it.

As time passed, Shannon and I got engaged. We were really in love with each other, and that love grew deeper and deeper. His daughter and my children all attended The Word Church together. It felt like we were a family. I was at a point in my life where I was tremendously happy.

The engagement to Shannon, and attending church regularly gave me a clearer understanding of what it meant to be a mother and a wife. I was truly getting in touch with parts of my spirituality that I'd never known existed. Both experiences were opening me up to new things and newfound happiness. I honestly hadn't felt that way since Darnell.

I was learning so much about myself. I learned my past didn't define who I am, nor did it define my future. The past mistakes I had made were just that—mistakes. As long as I learned from them, they could be stepping-stones to bigger and better things.

I also realized my few and far between prayers to God weren't enough. I needed to give Him *all* of me. I needed to give Him *all* of my heart and soul. I owed Him much more of my time, so I began going to church every Sunday, faithfully.

Admittedly, promising to give myself to God also posed a slight dilemma. The pastor preached about shacking up, playing house, and sex before marriage. I felt hypocritical sitting there with Shannon, knowing we were doing exactly what the pastor preached against. I knew premarital sex was wrong. I really started to dwell on it so much so that I tried to withhold sex from Shannon until we got married. In all honesty, I tried my hardest. I really did. But I'm only human. The withholding didn't last too long. Just like everyone else, I was a work in progress.

For the most part, I was successfully becoming a better mother, daughter, sister, and friend. I was growing smarter and gaining more control over my life and future. I was becoming more courageous and confident. I was beginning to see myself as a queen rather than just a woman. I began speaking differently, and became more eager to also listen and learn from others. I was becoming an all-around better person. I'd even stopped drinking. The deliverance of alcohol was needed.

I also matured in my understanding of death. I realized there was nothing I could've done the day of Darnell's death to prevent it. It was God's plan. It wasn't my fault, nor was it my fault that my nephew had died. I realized that when God decides He's ready to call us home, there's nothing any of us can do to stop it. The realizations made me finally bury the guilt of wishing I hadn't let Darnell leave out on that fateful day, or wishing I had watched my nephew that night like my sister had asked me to.

The Word Church is a place and a home that I *am* and always *will* be grateful for. It came into my life at a time when I really was searching for direction. The church made me a better person and a better human being, affirming my existing belief that God is real and He would never leave me.

❧ **CHAPTER 12** ❧

STRUGGLE

The struggle you're in today is prepping you for the strength you'll need tomorrow. Dispose of negative thoughts and replace them with positive ones. Think about how your testimony will later help some one else.

Ebony's Life Lesson #13

BY ANY MEANS

Memories are strange. As you're creating them, you have no idea that's what they will eventually become. When you're in a particular moment it doesn't cross your mind that it will quickly pass, and you'll never get it back. It doesn't occur to you that you will one day look back on that moment wishing you could return to it. That realization is a sad one. The passing of moments hit me hard when my aunt Diane was diagnosed with breast cancer.

She noticed a lump in her breast several times. She assumed it was only a cyst because it would come and go often, and didn't tell anyone about it. Aunt Diane thought it was nothing to worry about. In late 2010, the lump in her breast came back. This time, instead of disappearing, it remained, growing harder and more painful. Eventually the lump got so painful that she had to go to the emergency room and find out exactly what was going on. After a few x-rays, she was told the lump was cancerous.

I was devastated. Diane was my favorite aunt. She was the one who introduced me to having fun and enjoying life. She was my diva. She was the woman I wanted to be exactly like when I was growing up. The memories of happy times flooded my mind. I could remember all the parties, the smoking sessions, and the laughter and smiles we shared. It hurt my heart to know that all those moments with her could possibly come to an end.

As if it were a reflex, I dropped to my knees and prayed for my aunt with everything inside me. I prayed for her harder than I'd ever prayed for myself. From that point, I became her support system. I wasn't going to let her face her fight alone.

Aunt Diane was stubborn. That trait ran in my family. She hated having to go to her doctor's appointments. Sometimes she dug her heels in and refused to go, so I would have to ride her back at times and force her. Once we got there, as we usually did when we were together, we'd turn it into a party. We laughed. We joked. We smiled. We had fun; anything to keep her mind off of the depressing moment at hand.

Despite our laughter, there were times when I would somberly gaze at my aunt, worried that our good times were coming closer to an end. And because of my relationship with God, I sometimes wondered if she'd made her peace with Him. During her treatment, one of our cousins passed away. Aunt Diane and I attended the funeral together. Near the end of the service, the pastor said to the congregation, "If there's any time to get saved, it's now." He said none of us knew exactly when we are going to pass away; none of us know our time. He encouraged us all to get saved, accepting Jesus Christ as our Lord and Savior, before it was too late.

As people began to stand, Aunt Diane remained seated. I wanted her to stand badly. After several moments, the pastor said he could feel that there were more who should stand. He expressed that no one should be ashamed, shy, or embarrassed. I began to nudge my aunt. Seconds later, she stood. I was so proud of her. Of all the times I'd looked up to her and had admired her, I had never looked up to her more than at that moment.

"Thank you, Jesus," I whispered as tears fell from my eyes. I was so proud of her.

My auntie and I had lived crazy lives up until that point. We'd pushed life to the limit as far as we could. We had some reckless times and eventually, I was going to miss them all. At the moment she stood and got saved, I knew without a shadow of a doubt, this life was only the beginning. No matter what happened here on Earth, I would see her again on the other side.

I learned that all good things eventually come to an end. Happy moments eventually become sad ones and those who make you smile will inevitably make you cry. My relationship with Shannon was beginning to prove that.

The honeymoon stage of our relationship was over, and somehow, we began to grow apart. We were now beginning to argue. We could no longer see eye to eye. Eventually, we just couldn't get along anymore. It broke my heart. It broke his. What had started out so promising had now become a situation Shannon and I wished we hadn't ventured into. We were at each other's throats so badly that my oldest son had expressed how tired he was of our fighting. It reminded him of my relationship with Shawn, and he was now at the age where he would fight for his mother if he had to. He and Shannon would eventually butt heads. I couldn't have that. I didn't want him or my other babies to ever see anything resembling what they experienced during my relationship with Shawn. It was at that point that I realized it was over. I loved Shannon. He was my heart, but being together any longer just wasn't for us.

We broke up.

Once again I was completely on my own. It was difficult. I was only receiving $1,000 per month in survivor's benefits from Darnell, plus food stamps. In the beginning, I had no idea where my children and I were going to move. Knowing that I had nowhere else to go made me stick with Shannon a little while after I realized it wasn't going to work. Finally, my sister came through for me. She knew someone who was renting a house for an affordable price. The children and I moved in.

Moving into that house, and escaping from another failed relationship, made me think. I didn't like the conclusions I'd come to. I realized that this was the tenth home I'd moved into within the last ten years. Our lives, especially my children's, had become a cycle of packing and unpacking, putting things in storage, switching schools, making new friends, witnessing arguments and fighting. There was no stability. My babies were now fifteen, twelve, nine, and eight years old. They deserved better.

Financially, Shawn helped out specifically with Shawn Jr. on a regular basis. He always sent money, but rarely spent any time with him since he lived in Texas. He rarely visited Cleveland, which meant I was the mother and father to all of my children. It hurt me deeply that Shawn Jr. was my only child who had a living father, yet he never saw him. That reality broke my heart at times. Of course I wanted Shawn to be a father to his child and to be active in his life. But sadly, my other children would have to miss out on that experience. Since Darnell was dead, they wouldn't get a chance to find out what it was like to have that type of relationship. It was sad, and I could see the pain on their faces.

Since money was tight, my other three children really felt the pinch. Shawn always made sure his son had nice clothes and new sneakers. But since I was struggling financially, my other children didn't receive those luxuries. They had to go without new sneakers. They had to go without new clothes. I found a few odd jobs, but minimum wage just wasn't cutting it. Shannon would also come by often and hit me off with a few hundred dollars as a friendly gesture; never asking for it back. But that wasn't enough.

Often, there wasn't enough food to get us through the month. The electric bill would sometimes have to be neglected in order to pay the gas; leaving us with no lights. Or, I'd pay the electric bill instead, leaving us with no heat in the middle of winter. Ironically, this is how I had grown up. I realized this struggle wasn't normal or what God had planned for my life.

All of it shamed me. I wanted to break the cycle, changing my family's destiny forever. The most terrible feeling for a mother is not being able to truly provide for her children. It's easy to say material things aren't everything—when you have them. Try enduring the pain in your child's face when you have to tell them 'no' each time an event arises that requires money such as the circus, the movies, or Christmas. It shatters a parent's heart. Although they didn't have much and I knew it, I always made them feel like they had the world. I would go without, sacrificing things I wanted so they could have what they needed. Once, I went with two pair of jeans for six months and gave myself kitchen perms and homemade hairdos just to save for the children. That's why I did what I felt I had to do.

I don't condone drug dealing. I don't recommend it to anyone. All I know is it seemed like my only option at the time, although I knew it was wrong. Before I did it, I prayed to God that He would forgive me and that He would cloak me in His protection. From that point, I went for what I knew.

A friend of mine put me down with some Ecstasy pills and taught me the game. I wasn't proud at all. If anything, selling drugs made me feel like a failure. I felt like someone my children couldn't look up to. Embarrassed, I refused to let anyone in the family see me selling. I didn't want them to know. I saw drugs destroy far too many people's lives, whether using or selling. The last thing I wanted my babies to see was what I was doing, and to think it was okay for them to use drugs or to sell them.

Financially, things began to turn around for us. Selling drugs allowed me to catch up on my bills. The rent was paid; I could dress my babies in nice clothes, and always keep money in my pocket. As I was selling, I couldn't stop thinking about what God thought of me. I knew I had to be a disappointment to Him. I knew there was no way He would condone me selling poison. I prayed for forgiveness as often as possible. I prayed that God would send me something that would possibly save me from the choice I felt my current circumstances had forced me into.

During this time, Shannon and I, although just friends, were still sexing off and on when he came to town. He was still special to me. Other men were merely flings and one-night stands. Still, I had no intentions of taking a chance on going through with any of them what I'd gone through with Shawn. My defenses were still up. The only males I could give my heart to were my sons.

I also started to spend a lot of time with my grandmother. Time and age had caught up with her. She'd been having issues with her muscles and joints for several months. Then after seeing several doctors, she stopped. She refused to focus on her health from that point on. Because of that, her muscles eventually locked together and grew into an awkward, stuck position. She had no choice but to go see a doctor then. They told her she needed knee surgery. She refused mainly out of the fear of having someone cut her. The decision rendered her bedridden.

Seeing my grandmother in that state weighed heavily on my heart. I could still see her young, vibrant face and active body from past memories. I remembered how she always came through our family in a pinch. I could still see in my head how strong she had always been. Now, all of those moments were gone. She could no longer take care of herself. She could no longer walk. She could no longer provide. Her independence was gone.

My grandmother cried often, regretting her decision to avoid surgery. At times, she would actually say she wanted to die. She just couldn't take living out the rest of her life not being able to do for herself. It was torture for her, but we all stepped in to take care of her. The help embarrassed her. She was ashamed to have to be bathed, and being unable to use the bathroom on her own. She would cry her eyes out during some of those times. It was so humiliating to her. We still held her down.

I pulled closer to my kids just as I was pulling closer to my grandmother. Life and good health weren't promised, I realized. I showered my babies with my love while once again reflecting hard on my life. Selling drugs had me at a crossroads. I wanted to stop. I needed to stop. But going back to struggling to pay the bills frightened me. Eventually, I realized if I kept going, the police would either catch me or I'd die, leaving my kids as wards of the state. The game was never fair to anyone. If either of those things happened, what would my children be left with? With all that weighing on my mind, I decided the final bag of pills I had left of my supply would be my last. I would be turning thirty-five within two weeks and wanted to celebrate with a clean slate. I was going to leave the drugs behind, and pray that God had something else in store for me. Little did I know, He did.

┌─────────────────────────────────┐
│   │
│   ‹ **CHAPTER 13** ›   │
│   │
│   THINGS GET BETTER   │
│   │
│   *With faith, hope and a prayer anything is* │
│   *possible. When praying, you have to hope that* │
│   *things are going to get better.* │
│   │
│   *Ebony's Life Lesson #14* │
│   │
└─────────────────────────────────┘

VANTAGE POINT

It started out as a normal day. It was a Saturday night—my birthday weekend. The thought of turning thirty-five in two days excited me to the core. I kept having these weird feelings that something new was in store for me. It was as if my spirit wanted to tell me something. My entire demeanor had changed over the last few weeks, just wanting to do better in life. I wanted to give up selling drugs and the constant drinking, and spend as much time with my children as possible. I'd spent most of the day cleaning the house, watching TV, and cooking. When a family friend called me saying they were going out to a new spot that had recently opened, everything changed. My first thought was, *tonight's not the night.* It was a relaxation night, a night where I needed to chill. My spirit urged me to stay inside.

Darnell Jr. didn't waste any time making his opinion clear. He didn't want me to go out, saying he didn't want his mother at a bar since his uncle had recently been murdered while out partying. To the contrary, Dariell pushed for me to go, citing reasons why I deserved a girl's night out. "You need some time to yourself," she told me. "Go ahead, enjoy yourself."

Before long, India and I had talked about the possible plans. At that point, I heard everyone out, and decided to get dressed. The plan was for us to leave from India's house so that we could all ride together. We planned to hit up two or three places to see where we'd end up. My hair was flawless, and I slipped on a long, blue maxi dress, feeling like a queen inside and out. If only we had the ability to know when something dreadful is coming our way, maybe then we could be better prepared for the occasion.

We arrived at the first spot, had a great time, and moved on to the next location. My family truly knew how to bring in a birthday. We even stopped by a local club where Brains was hosting a party. He had no idea I was coming, but of course, he was happy to see me. For some reason, I couldn't shake him totally. We didn't stay long. I chatted with Brains for a bit, loving the way he made me feel, and then left.

Our bar hopping continued until I suddenly felt the need to go home. No one in my circle wanted to leave. They were having a good time. When my cousin Dominique asked me why I wanted to end the night early, it was hard to explain. There really wasn't a reason. I simply wanted to go home.

While they understood, they kept partying. Immediately, I texted Brains, *I'm at The Touch of Italy. Come pick me up.*

He responded that he'd wrap things at the party, and come. The party and the fun continued as I waited for him. He never came, and eventually Dominique, Demetria, and India were ready to leave. They had decided to turn in too, but felt like they were too intoxicated to drive me all the way home. Each person had an excuse as why they didn't take me home, but nonetheless, everything happens for a reason.

* * *

We were all tipsy, laughing, and enjoying ourselves as we climbed into the car, and headed back to my sister's house. The night had been more than fun and I wanted to go home. But no one wanted to take me home at that moment. Since I wasn't driving, I had to go with the flow.

With the music playing, we turned off Kinsman Ave and onto my sister's street. As we approached India's driveway, we noticed a car parked in her spot. We had never seen it before and had no idea why it was there. As we reached the end of the driveway, we could see about four or five people sitting in the car. They appeared to be females.

Needing to pull into the driveway, Dominique blew the horn. Each of us could see movement inside but the driver refused to back out. We blew the horn more and more and then yelled toward the car. Still, the driver didn't back out.

Inside our car, we all said a few things amongst ourselves, some rational words and some more cruel. The females simply wouldn't leave, causing Dominique to drive two houses down to our grandmother's house for the time being.

Afterward, we got out, headed down the sidewalk to India's house and approached the parked car. As we walked down the street, I knew things could get ugly. Was this why I felt that I needed to stay at home with my children? Whatever the case, it was way too late. Somewhere in between the name-calling, and taunts toward India, the car backed out of India's driveway and into the driveway directly across the street. They simply would not leave.

The dispute began quickly and exploded even quicker. We were all caught off guard by the argument between my family and the girls in the unwelcomed car. Needless to say, we shouted back to the group of girls trespassing in our neighborhood. The doors of their car opened quickly, and all five females hopped out. The fuse had been lit, and so many different accounts have been told since then. One thing is for certain; everyone met in the middle of the street and began taunting each other with words flying back and forth. Suddenly, catching me completely off guard, one of the girls from the car punched me. Out of reflex, I swung back even though I didn't want any problems. I'd been through enough pain in life already.

All hell broke loose.

We were all brawling in the middle of the street. Punches and kicks were being thrown in all directions. Over a bunch of yelling and name-calling, the girls headed back to their car. Threats were still being made from both sides but only out of anger. The girls finally climbed back into the car. Seconds later, one of them threw a bottle from their car window, targeted at me. It missed and shattered in the street.

The moment that followed changed my life and will haunt my dreams until the day I die. It was at that moment that I had realized why my sixth sense had given me such a bad feeling about going out that night.

The engine of the car revved up, and a second later, it sped out of the driveway. As it did, the driver purposely jerked the steering wheel in my direction even though she had plenty of space to go in any direction she wanted. She had the choice of going either left, or right, instead of coming directly towards me. As the headlights bore down on me, in a split second, I saw the many flashes of pain in my life: the man forcing me to do sexual things to him at a young age, the fists of the man I once loved crashing into my face, the fists of the men my mother loved crashing into hers, the knife intentionally forced into her chest, the stench of the man who raped me in that bathroom at fourteen, the day my father moved out, the day I became a widow with three children to feed, and so much more.

Each moment blazed by in blinding flashes. The pain of each moment rushed me. I guess it was an act to instantly prepare me for the pain I was about to face.

The car slammed into me. Immediately, the force made me crumple over the hood and my hands crashed down on its surface. At that moment...

Darkness.

I can't remember anything about that night from then on.

Now, I know the specific accounts that have been told to me by India, who was on the scene of the incident, my mother, Rose, who saw me the first time in the hospital, and Shannon, who ended up at the emergency room before the ambulance could get me there.

India's Story

"You have to survive for your kids, Ebony," I can still hear myself saying that night with tears in my eyes.

Watching her lying on the ground was the darkest dread I had ever experienced. My ears can still hear the screams. My eyes can still see the long, wide trail of fresh blood that stained the street. I can still remember my sister's grotesque body lying on the ground, not moving. That night will never leave me. I'm still amazed by how quickly laughter can turn into tears. It's even more amazing how just in the blink of an eye a life can be changed so drastically.

Before long, I realized it was my ex's girlfriend who yelled out something disrespectful from the car that was parked in our driveway. At first, I had no idea she was sitting inside. I also didn't know why she was coming at me in such a foul way. I admit the two of us had a fight the previous Thanksgiving, but we squashed that. We were good as far as I knew.

Feeling extremely disrespected, I yelled back, "Don't disrespect my house!"

As this was happening, we all made our way down the street. Next thing we knew, all five girls jumped out of the car, approaching me. Refusing to back down, I stood my ground. I wasn't going to run. They were in the wrong, not me.

Words were exchanged. Ebony got between us and tried to be the peacemaker. She tried her best to diffuse the situation. Suddenly all five girls jumped on Ebony. They were hitting her as hard as they could with their fists. Immediately, I jumped in to defend my sister. Seconds later, my cousins came running up the street. Before long it was a free-for-all. We were in the middle of the street fighting.

As we fought, my uncle and nephew came out of my house, darted towards us, and attempted to break up the fight. They never hit any of the girls that we were fighting. They were simply trying to separate us all.

Over a bunch of yelling and name calling, the girls headed back to their car. Threats were made from both sides, but only out of anger at the moment. The girls jumped back into the car. Seconds later, one of them threw a bottle of liquor out of the window at us. One of us threw a flowerpot back at them. The moment that followed changed my life, Ebony's, and everyone close to us, forever.

The engine of the car revved up and it mowed down Ebony's body. But my mind hadn't registered what happened. It was strange. I mean, all I knew was one second she was standing there and the next she was gone. It happened so fast. It was so unbelievable and so unimaginable. My mind didn't grasp what had happened.

Pandemonium broke loose. That was when my mind deciphered what happened. The car had run my sister over. Along with my family, I ran out into the street to see the car headed up the block. My sister's body was slowing it down. She was trapped underneath.

"Stop!" everyone yelled horrifically. "Stop!"

The driver of the car didn't stop. She continued to gas the engine and drag my sister. It was the most horrifying sight I had ever seen. Finally the car reached the corner and made a right turn. As it did, my sister's body tore loose from the undercarriage. It flipped and rolled over the street top a few times and then came to rest as the car sped off.

My family and I reached Ebony in a brief second, although it felt like forever to get to her. Each step didn't seem like it would ever get us there. Although everything happened so fast, it seemed to be going in slow motion. When I reached my sister, I couldn't believe what I saw.

Ebony was lying on the ground with her arms and legs twisted in unnatural positions. One of her legs was actually touching her back. Portions of her flesh were ripped open. Blood was spilling from her. A trail of it led from where the car first hit her all the way to where she was now lying.

"Ebony!" we all screamed as our eyes took in what was lying at our feet.

Ebony didn't answer. She didn't even move. She just laid still. We all gathered around her, yelling and screaming hysterically.

"Give her room to breathe!" my cousin Dominique screamed. "She needs air. Back up!"

We all backed away, but not too far. Chaos had been unleashed among us. We cried. We screamed. We watched with wide eyes. We paced back and forth. Our hearts were broken. Our worlds were crumbling.

Neighbors ran out of their houses, rushing toward us. Dominique, who had medical experience, told one of them to bring as many towels and sheets as possible.

Ebony was bleeding heavily; it wouldn't stop flooding from her body. She was going to bleed to death if my sister didn't get the rags to stop the bleeding.

I collapsed to the ground in tears. My knees couldn't hold me up. I could no longer walk. From the ground, I watched as Dominique held my sister's still body and whispered things to her, hoping she would respond. Ebony never did. Her unresponsiveness made me think the absolute worst. I thought my sister was dead.

So many tears streamed down my face. They clouded my vision. Everything around me was spinning. In my head, I could see me and my sister playing as kids. I could see all the fun times we had. I could see the smiles and hear the laughter. I could see the celebration we just had for her at the club. It terrified me that all those things and experiences would never happen again. It made me hysterical.

It seemed like an eternity for the ambulance to get there. When I first heard its approaching sirens, as they grew near, they still just seemed so far away, so distant. The ambulance arrived quickly, but the wait seemed so much longer. As its red lights poured onto the street and illuminated houses, faces and front yards, my sister still hadn't spoken. She still hadn't moved.

Finally, I got up, made my way to her, knelt beside her body and told her, "Ebony, you've got to make it. You've got to make it for your kids. You've got to fight. They need you."

Ebony stirred for the first time since she had been lying there. But just as quickly as the stirring began, it abruptly stopped. She went totally still again. Moments later, she was being placed into the back of the

139

ambulance. The rest of us stood there with uncertainty. We had no idea if she would leave us or if she had *already* left us. As the ambulance turned on its sirens and sped off, all any of us knew, at that moment, was that our lives would ever be the same again.

Shannon's Story

Ebony's accident was something I've tried to erase from my mind. It was the most horrific thing I had ever seen in my life. Ebony and three of her family members had come by to see me at a club that night. I'd only seen her for about fifteen minutes, and then they left. It was cool to see her.

Later, I got a text from Eb from a different number. She asked if I would come get her from The Touch of Italy. She was ready to go home, and the other ladies weren't. I couldn't make it to where she was at the time. But I did end up heading that way to get her. When I got to The Touch, she was gone. I texted her back to see if she was okay but I didn't get a response.

I called the number back that she texted me from and I heard her sister screaming. She just kept screaming Ebony's name over and over. When I asked what happened, she told me that Ebony was hit by a car. I couldn't understand. I just saw her. She told me Ebony was taken to Metro Health Hospital, so I headed there.

When I got to the hospital, I paced the hallways, looking in rooms, thinking about what India told me. I got to one hallway, and a doctor was standing there.

I asked the doctor about Ebony Canion, but the doctor didn't know who she was. At this time she hadn't been identified, so I told him that she was just been hit by a car. He realized whom I was talking about, and braced me for what I was about to see. When I went in the room, I couldn't believe it.

She looked like a piece of bloody meat, lying on a table, lifeless. Everything was swollen, so big as if someone pumped air into her body. I just knew she was dead.

I just saw her an hour before. I knew her body well, so I knew it was Ebony, but she looked nothing like herself. Her face was wide open, and I could literally see the inside of her mouth. Her legs were twisted. She had big gashes on her side. She didn't show any signs of life.

The doctors had pretty much given up. They were in awe. I'm the type of guy that gets queasy looking at small things. But God works in certain situations. He numbed me to my normal queasiness.

I went over to Eb and said, "Ebony, these people are giving up on you. You've got to show them something. Give them a sign." Then, I saw her blink.

It's crazy because that made her fight. I told the doctors, "Look, she's responding!" They rushed me out of there, and I'm guessing that was when her first of several surgeries began. I felt the need to be there for her. I wanted her to fight because I knew she would do the same for me.

My Mother's Story

I got a call at 3 a.m. It was my daughter, India. She was screaming through the phone, "Ma, Ebony…Ebony…Ebony…Ebony."

She was crying, and I didn't understand what she was saying. She said, "I need to get to the hospital!" Panicked, I called my brother-in-law, John. I didn't know what happened, all I knew was that Ebony was being taken to the hospital. He was supposed to pick me up, but never came.

In all of the confusion, I had forgotten that my other daughter, Charmaine, lived around the corner from me. I called her. She immediately started crying, and telling me that Ebony had been run over by a car. She told me that Ebony may not make it, and that we needed to get there, fast. I got dressed and rushed downstairs from my apartment. I came outside, and paced back and forth waiting for Charmaine to come. It seemed like an eternity before she finally showed up.

"Ma, you gotta drive," she told me. I was crying, barely able to understand her. "Ma, I can't drive on the freeway."

Ebony was taken to a hospital on the West side, so I got behind the wheel, and headed there. Frantic at first, I pulled myself together so we could get there safely.

When I arrived at the hospital, there were so many people standing outside, including my sister, and the father of India's children who was extremely upset.

"Why did they do this?" he asked angrily. He threw his cell phone down in disgust.

I walked past the crowd and into the hospital. I was led to a waiting room where the rest of my family waited. They were crying. I didn't know how bad things were until they began to tell that Ebony was hit by a car. They said the car dragged her, and after her lifeless body had fallen from underneath the car, it kept on going. I started crying, and can't remember stopping for a long time. Maybe about an hour later, the doctors came in and told me it was pretty bad. We waited another hour until they told me, "You can see your daughter."

I remember looking at Ebony when I walked in, and saying, "Oh, my God!" She was about three times larger than her normal size. She was unrecognizable. Shortly after, the doctors said they wanted to talk to me. The doctors told me bluntly that she was in critical condition, and that she may not make it. I rushed back out to the waiting room, and sat there for a minute, trying to gather my confused thoughts before going outside to privately say a prayer. After that, I knew it was time to go talk to Ebony. I knew she was unconscious, but I spoke to her anyway.

"Ebony, you're strong. You're a strong woman. You're going to make it. I know you are."

I never gave up hope.

❧ CHAPTER 14 ☙

RESILIENCE

*There are so many of us who've we've been
through the unthinkable and we've still managed
to bounce back. If you survived whatever
victimized you, I want to salute you, my fellow
survivor. You are amazing and you wear the title
well!*

Ebony's Life Lesson #15

A SURVIVOR IS BORN

They say the things that we go through in life mold us into the people we become.

Our trials and tribulations give us strength, and prepare us for what's ahead. It was clear that my life had been heavily laced with darkness. My heart had been broken, and shattered into countless, jagged shards on numerous occasions. My trust has been betrayed. Yes, there had been splashes of happiness here and there, but darkness became more of a constant companion to me than the good times.

I once heard an elderly person say, "Life is sometimes hard, but it's fair." I never quite understood that saying when I was younger. I didn't understand what was so fair about what I was going through. Now, I understand it all clearly. You see, every one of us has to pay a fee to walk God's Earth, to breathe His air and to receive His blessings. None of us are exempt. We all have to earn our keep, whether it's in pain, struggle, losing loved ones, or anything else that hurts us. I understand that now. I just wonder why my fee always seemed to be steeper than most.

Upon arriving at the hospital, from what I'm told, my family braced themselves for the worst. After all, they witnessed something so grotesque and inhumane, something that a family should never have to endure. It didn't take a rocket scientist to know my chances of surviving my injuries were slim. In all honesty, they were expecting that night to end with them saying their final goodbyes.

I can't imagine what a horrific sight it must've been for my family to see me that way, especially the very first night of the accident. So much of my skin had been stripped away, leaving me unrecognizable.

I've been told that I no longer resembled the person I used to be in any shape or form; I looked more like a bloody slab of meat. My body was three to four times its normal size due to extreme swelling. Large patches of my scalp and hair were literally ripped from my head while other patches of skin were ripped from my face and body. Nearly severed completely, my tongue needed to be sewn back on, and my mouth was ripped open. Several teeth were gone. Bones were broken and crushed, exposed by wide-open gashes and rips that tore all the way down to the bone. Bloodstained gauze bandages covered me. Tubes hung from my mouth, helping me to breathe, while others dangled from my arms. God, I shudder just thinking about it.

I don't know how I would've coped with seeing someone I loved hurt that way, especially when I think

146

about what it must've been like for my mother. I was her second born. We have been through so much together. Our bond was deep, so I know it must've been torture for her to see her baby in such a terrible state, and to know there was nothing she could do to take the pain away. All she could do was pray. There wasn't a guarantee that her child would survive. My knees get weak just imagining where I would get the strength to bear the experience if it were *me* standing beside my child's bed.

For my loved ones, the first night of sitting in that waiting room was filled with regrets, reflections, and tears. My mother told me that pain filled their hearts. Sadness was in their eyes and on their faces. Their regrets and what ifs plagued them, making the pain worse.

What if the girls hadn't convinced me to go out that night? What if someone called the police when the fight first broke out? Everyone wished they could have or would have done something differently.

Of course, spite and anger towards the girls who had done this to me filled them too. Memories of happier times filled their heads in an attempt to combat what they witnessed, and to help them cope with the strong possibility that I wasn't going to live.

From the moment I was rushed into the emergency room, my body didn't stir. My eyes didn't open. No words left my mouth. Nothing about me displayed life, or even an interest in making an attempt to grasp for life. The ventilator breathed for me, and from the outside, my family assumed I had given up. The odds were all stacked against me. The doctors were even preparing to give up since I was so unresponsive. My battle for another day on God's Earth was a silent one, and being fought behind the pitch-black darkness of my eyelids.

A lot was taken away from me up until the accident, particularly people I loved: my husband, father, the sister whom I never got to meet, and my nephew. Parts of my heart and soul had been taken by way of molestation, rape, and domestic abuse. I'd seen a lot and done a lot. But in spite of it all, I always found a way to fight through and come out on the other side as a better and stronger person. Now, I was in a fight beyond measure; a fight most didn't think I'd win…the fight for my life.

From the beginning, I wasn't expected to survive. If I did, I was expected to have brain damage.

Expected to never walk again.

Expected to never talk again.

My body was so badly damaged that each of those things were only estimates. If I were on the outside looking in at me, I would've thought the exact same thing. I seemed like a hopeless case; I was too damaged to be repaired. But as the old saying goes, 'It ain't always about the size of the dog in the fight, sometimes, it's about the size of the *fight* in the dog.'

Something inside wouldn't allow me to give up. The pain became unbearable, and worsened as the attempt to repair my body continued during those first few days. Eventually the doctors decided to put me into an induced coma and performed five different surgeries.

Not realizing I was in a coma at the time, I began dreaming and hallucinating about things going on around me. Some were pleasant, and others, not so much. I remember seeing visions of my son, and people touching me in a way that I hated, assuming it was more abuse. Somewhere in between the multiple surgeries, and the effort to save me, I had a vision of my back being sprayed down by a water hose in the burn unit. At the time, I didn't know what was going on. I assumed I was being abused. I thought they were trying to drown me. Yet, worse than the drowning, my heart shattered when visions of my mother dying entered my head. She was shot by the same people who put me in the hospital in the first place. Strangely, I even visualized her funeral.

As usual, my family pulled together and stood by my side as the nights turned into weeks. For the entire time I lay in that coma, they kept vigil, while taking care of my children and doing their best to keep my house running. I'm not entirely sure if they believed in their hearts I was going to make it. I only know that they hung in there with me and held me down, no matter what.

Day after day, my family stopped by to sit by my bed and pray for hours at a time. They whispered in my ear to let me know they were pulling for me, while also hoping that hearing their voices would give me strength. From what I've been told, I never responded. My body endured so much pain from the countless surgeries to repair and set broken bones, and numerous skin grafts to replace the skin on the areas where I lost flesh. Through each procedure, I remained in a coma.

My family grew more tormented as the days went on. There were so many unknown and unanswered questions. What exactly should they tell my grieving children? Would I live or die? If I lived, would I be mentally retarded? Would I ever be able to do any of the things that normal people do? Uncertainty plagued them, but they held on. Without their support, without their love and their words of inspiration, I don't know how things would've turned out.

Of course, it's obvious that God was looking down on me. I know in my heart that He kept his hand on me the entire time, from the moment the car hit me up until the present. I guess all those years of pulling close to Him in my many times of need had prepped my relationship with Him for that moment. Still, there was no certainty of what God had in store for me in the end. No promise of life or death. As nights and days passed by, I entered the second month in a coma. Once again, my family, my children and my friends, although supportive, had no choice but to hope and pray that I would find the strength to fight my way through. Little did they know I would need their prayers and a strength I didn't know I had in order to get me through much more than just a coma.

What lay ahead of me was going to be a hard-fought struggle.

℃ CHAPTER 15 ℰ

BEAUTY ON THE INSIDE

When you're beautiful on the inside there's no flaw or scar on the outside that can hide that beauty. Love the skin you're in! Embrace your different, embrace your flaws, embrace who you are and never ever forget that your image is just what God imagined.

Ebony's Life Lesson #16

MY BEAUTIFUL SCARS

Just like anyone else, specifically women, the looks and my outward appearance meant a lot to me. I had always taken pride in my body's curves, the length of my hair, the texture and richness of my skin, the brightness of my smile, and the size of my butt.

Somewhere during my young adult years, I'd even earned the nickname Big Booty Judy, a name that I hated. Thankfully, my father had always taught me there had to be more to a person than looks. I agreed, and had always tried to show people my inner beauty. "You have to be a great person on the inside," he preached. "God gave you a purpose in life and it's not found in looks." Grateful for my father's words, I was about to embrace them and live them.

Before long, the decision was made to bring me out of the coma. It was a process that required patience, medicine, and prayer. After almost two months, I was taken off the breathing tube, allowing my body to breathe independently and at its own pace. Although that took time, a glimmer of hope came when my mother recalls the moment tears ran down my face. She said I never spoke any words or showed any movement at that time, but just seeing the tears lifted everyone's spirits. Thinking back on it, I'm sure I must've been dreaming; possibly of my past struggles, or maybe they were tears of joy, knowing I had been called by a higher power to overcome and would end up as an inspiration to others like me.

That small sign encouraged the doctors and my family that I was progressing. Several weeks later, by the grace of God, I slowly began coming out of the coma. I remember waking up, unable to move from the neck down. Since my tongue was still swollen and filled with stitches, and there was a feeding tube in my mouth, I couldn't speak. I also had no feeling whatsoever in my hands, or my feet. It was an absolutely terrifying feeling. I remember hearing beeping sounds from the various machines and voices around me, causing me to open my eyes.

Charmaine sat close to me, rubbing my head, and my mother was also beside my bed. Both of their faces lit up when they saw my eyes open sluggishly. Then the screaming began. Calls and shouts for the doctor filled the room. I wondered what was going on, especially after seeing my mother's face. Since I dreamed that she was dead while in my coma, seeing her now, alive and breathing, frightened me. My brain couldn't quite understand why she was there. Of course, it felt great looking into her face, but my dream made the current moment seem surreal. It made me wonder if I was going crazy.

While my mother, sister, and the doctors made a big deal out of me opening my eyes, blurred thoughts flipped through my mind. I didn't know why I was in the hospital or why I couldn't move my body. Numerous questions filled me. Soon, I realized that a Foley catheter had been inserted through my urethra and into my bladder for my stool, along with a feeding tube for me to eat. The realization that I couldn't walk, or get up to use the bathroom freely hit me hard. My life had changed in the blink of an eye. I wanted to scream, but couldn't. I wanted to talk, and to reach out to my mother and sister, but couldn't. The feeling was both weird and terrifying.

As days passed, a lot of new information was being revealed to me. Still, I was kept in the dark about why I had to be admitted to the hospital in the first place. My family instantly lied, telling me we were in a car accident. I knew it wasn't true, but remained lethargic and in deep, confused thought.

During certain periods, some memories would trickle through my mind. In time, I remembered a fight, but couldn't recollect the details at first.

As time moved forward, I would recall different scenarios and ask my mother and sisters for verification, hoping for the truth. They would nod, but still wouldn't give me too much information until they realized I was beginning to remember more and more. I know now that they were trying to protect me. They didn't want me to suffer mentally, and most importantly, no one wanted me to see my face so soon.

Eventually I began to regain feeling in my hands, so I was given a pen and pad to write on. In the beginning, everything came out looking like gibberish. I was barely able to control my muscles. When I finally did, I asked for my cell phone, but no one would give it to me. At the time, their reasons went over my head. I eventually wrote about the dreams I had during my coma. As it turned out, some of what I thought were dreams were actual events. I realized that being sprayed down with that water hose while in the burn unit actually occurred. The hospital staff never abused me, as my coma-induced dreams would have me to believe. I obviously had some consciousness or memory of the nurse spraying me down, attempting to prevent infection.

I also told them I couldn't remember going underneath that car. I exhausted my brain on many days trying to remember. Picturing myself underneath the undercarriage of the car, and my back being skinned did something to me emotionally, damaging my mental recovery. Once that happened, my mother and sister decided it was time to tell me exactly what happened to me.

Hearing about the incident knocked me to a bad place mentally. I couldn't fathom that a car could hit and drag me almost two hundred feet. That was the type of thing that happened to *other* people. It couldn't have happened to me. It was difficult to accept, but I had no choice. The same way I had to accept seeing myself for the first time since the incident.

After feeling what I thought was a cold sore on my face, my nurse proceeded to give me some ointment. They were in cahoots, not wanting me to see what I actually looked like, thinking it would traumatize me. I couldn't get out of bed, so the only way to see myself would be from a mirror or from my cell phone camera, so keeping the phone away seemed to be a good plan. But after massaging and measuring the wounds on my face, I knew what I'd felt appeared to be bigger than a cold sore. I turned to my mother.

"Ma, please give me my phone."

At this point, my family knew it was time. By now, I'd already asked for it on several occasions. The tricks had gone on long enough. Turning the camera on my phone toward my face flipped my world upside down. My emotions took off for a ride; Shock, disbelief, sadness, powerlessness, and anger hit me all at once. I couldn't believe what I was seeing. Where had the old Ebony gone? Why did this have to happen to me? Why my face? I cried out, thinking about how my life would end up.

I assumed people would stare at me. I wondered if I would have to live my life with my face swollen and discolored. The right side of my face was bright pink and resembled a large zipper with extra-thick stiches. My forehead had changed to a reddish hue, and had also been stitched up. I wondered who would want me. Would my kids be embarrassed to be around me, or let people know I was their mother? Thoughts fired from left to right, causing me to emotionally break down, and forcing my family and doctors to reveal all details, and the extent of my injuries. They read like a laundry list: brain trauma, pelvic ring fracture, rods and screws were placed in my pelvis, acute respiratory failure, chest wall emphysema, fractured shoulder, a fracture in my left knee and ankle, rods were placed in my leg, dislocations in my spine, tongue lacerations, fractures in my ribs, liver injury, heavy blood loss, three missing teeth, and much, much, *much* more.

Honestly, hearing it all made me want to give up at that very moment. My entire universe darkened. I cried uncontrollably, feeling that there was no way in the world I would be able to overcome all of those injuries. I couldn't see myself ever walking again or talking again. I couldn't see myself having an enjoyable future. I felt so depressed and miserable. My situation seemed far too hopeless. Even attempting to move forward seemed so pointless.

I thought about my grandmother, and how one of the saddest things I ever witnessed was watching her go from being such a strong independent woman to becoming completely helpless; having to depend on those around her for *everything*. She felt more like a burden than a human being. Now I was faced with those same challenges.

My recovery process, which is still in progress, began as a humiliating and painful one. At times it was pure hell. I started out as if I was a newborn baby. I didn't know how to talk, or eat. I couldn't hold my bowels. I couldn't walk. I couldn't sit up. I was completely weak and helpless. So just like a newborn baby, I had to learn and progress one step at a time. But know this, with God, ANYTHING is possible.

I fought through the humiliation. Even the word embarrassment can't define what I was feeling during those certain moments. Imagine having someone else, most times a stranger, seeing you naked and having to bathe you because you can't clean yourself. Imagine having someone else having to assist you in doing some of the most personal things, such as relieving your bladder. It felt horrible to me. I couldn't even chew food properly; it hurt too badly from the lacerations on my tongue.

One of the most shameful and embarrassing moments of my recovery was my difficulty controlling my bowels. In the beginning, I couldn't control them at all. I would have accidents often, and my nurses would have to clean me up. As they did, I can't explain how dirty and humiliated I felt. I didn't even want to show my face. It made me cry my eyes out at times. It also brought back the memories of my grandmother's struggle. I could remember her crying in the bathtub. I could remember the pain on her face and in her eyes. Now I knew exactly what it must've been like for her. Now I knew how much it must've hurt. That same shame dwelled inside of me, and often pushed me when my motivation was low.

Sadly, as I laid in my coma before the recovery process, my grandmother lost her battle with her health. She passed away. Sometimes I wonder if it was her health that killed her, or was it the broken heart which was brought on by having to spend the rest of her life in such a helpless state. I wonder if she just couldn't take it anymore and gave up.

Missing her, I vowed to not give up. My determined spirit kicked in, coupled with the constant motivation of others around me. My family and friends played a huge part in the long recovery ahead. They were always there assisting in any way possible. Shannon was one of those friends who was always there, remained by my side often. He'd make me laugh at moments when joy was the furthest thing from my mind and heart. He'd make me smile when I honestly didn't feel like it. When I was finally able to move to a hospital better suited for my recovery, he'd lift me from my bed and into a wheelchair, and push me on wild rides up and down the hospital's hallways. I'm forever grateful to him for everything he did. He was, and still is, a great friend, despite the fact that we were no longer in a committed relationship.

Of course my mother and my sisters were by my side also. They were always praying for me and encouraging me. They were always telling me I could beat my current circumstances if I fought hard and stayed focused. I'll always love them for that.

One day, they told me, I would become an inspiration to so many people because of my will to fight for life and recovery. I liked that feeling. Inside, I wanted people to someday say, "Because of you, I didn't give up."

And because of you, I won't give up.

Of course, my fight to get back was a difficult one. Just learning to lift up in my bed became an extreme battle. It seemed impossible in the beginning, but eventually I made it happen. Once that was achieved, I could be placed in a wheelchair and then begin other aspects of my recovery, such as learning to stand, to coordinate my body movements, and even learning to speak clearly again. But it was all coming at very slow and tedious pace. Sometimes it seemed like forever. But I remained determined.

The battle to get well was also agonizing. I mean really *painful*. The discomfort and agony was unbearable at times. Since the numerous bones in my body that had been fractured had been unused for so long and were all in various stages of healing, putting weight on them, or simply trying to move them hurt terribly. It was beyond pain. Sometimes just the slightest movement would bring me to tears. It hurt that bad. Also, I had to go through more surgeries. The pain of it all sent me through stints where I often wanted to give up, but I had to force my way through. I realized that *survivor spirit* had gotten to me.

During this time, I learned just how much the small things in life really mean. As living, breathing creatures, we tend to take so many minor things in life for granted; like stubbing your toe, sitting on your front porch, opening your refrigerator, picking up the phone to call a family member, and so much more. I'm no different. Up until that moment, I had taken all those things for granted too. I never paid any attention to how valuable those things were because they never seemed to be significant. I guess it's easy to feel that way when you have good health, and everything seems to be normal. But now I was in a position where I could no longer experience those things and I missed them terribly. It terrified me that I would possibly *never* be able to experience them again.

Eventually during my recovery, I was moved again, this time to a rehabilitation hospital. They were better equipped to deal with my injuries and recovery process. Finally, I could be wheeled outside in my wheelchair. I can't even begin to describe how amazing it felt to have the sun touch the surface of my skin, or how it felt to breathe fresh air. It had been months since the unexpected trauma on my body. I missed the outdoors. I missed seeing the trees and hearing the birds chirping. I missed hearing and seeing cars ride up and down the street. Being able to once again experience those things—God's creations—meant the world to me.

God, thank you. Even in my dark days of recovery, I realized He'd given me a second chance at life. I took it, grabbed the task by the horns, and worked hard at rebuilding my body.

Soon, I graduated to physical therapy involving parallel bars to learn how to stand again and to attempt to walk. It was hard to do in the beginning. My feet and bones couldn't bear weight. They were still too weak and in various stages of healing, so they were very fragile. It was a challenge at times that I didn't think I was up for. Eventually though, with persistence and God's grace, I moved forward and advanced to being able to walk with a walker. I was so proud of myself, and thought back to a motivational piece embedded in my mind.

Things may seem as if they aren't moving fast enough for you, and as if you're at a standstill in life. Your steps feel huge, but the goal ahead still seems so far away. Don't second-guess yourself. DON'T GIVE UP NOW! Keep fighting! Things may be slow, but sometimes, the longer progress takes, the longer it lasts, and the more you'll appreciate it! Be patient! Every achievement happens when it's supposed to.

Another achievement that meant so much to me was finally learning to control my bowels. That was a relief. In the beginning, the doctors kept suggesting I have an ostomy bag attached to me. I refused each time. I couldn't fathom spending the rest of my life needing a bag. In my heart I knew my bowels would finally kick in like they were supposed to. My will to control them pushed forward. Finally, the hard work paid off and I learned to control them. My nurses were wonderful. They always made me feel better and were a large part of my recovery. We would sit and talk about everything, not only my physical progress, but my personal life as well. They were almost like a second family to me.

Each achievement, no matter how small or big, meant the world to me. I felt like I was defying the odds. I wasn't supposed to have survived the tragic incident, but I did. I wasn't supposed to walk again, but I was taking steps. My tears of pain were becoming tears of joy. I felt so proud of myself and so happy to be alive.

Prayers really do work.

God is real.

And He is a healer.

❧ CHAPTER 16 ❧

BE AWARE

The devil usually strikes right before your biggest breakthrough. He wants nothing more than to see us hurt and doubting God. He knows us well and he will use what he knows against us. So be aware of the devil just as you are aware of God.

Ebony's Life Lesson #17

THE POWER OF PRAYER

There comes a time in our lives when we have to recognize the very moment where God is giving us a chance to restart life with a clean slate. There comes a moment when you have to place everything behind you, and focus on what's ahead of you. For me, my clean slate began the moment I was wheeled out of the hospital and was finally able to go home. Before that, I felt within my heart that I really needed to make good on some things.

First, I prayed to God my most ultimate and heartfelt prayer. I gave immense thanks to Him for not only giving me the strength to make it this far, but also for life itself. Everything He'd given me, whether in material things or experience, good or bad, was greatly appreciated and would never be taken for granted again. I also prayed for forgiveness for all things I'd done in the past. Then, knowing the journey ahead of me would be a difficult one, I prayed that He would give me the strength to face everything, no matter how difficult, with my head up.

The second thing I did was reflect on all the bad things that I had done in my life, and also the people I'd hurt, knowingly and unknowingly. I didn't want to have anyone angry with me. Not saying I was an angel all my life, but in all honesty, there was only one person whom I could think of that I really hurt. I reached out to that person and made amends. From there, it was time to take the journey home. It was finally time to face the first day of the rest of my life. First though, the devil, as usual, showed his ugly head. I should've expected it.

A few weeks before leaving the hospital, the prosecutor for my case came to visit me. Up until that point, I hadn't thought about the woman who actually hit me. The focus had been more on getting well. I guess that's why it shocked me when the prosecutor recanted the version of that night's events from the girls who ran me over. None of what they said made any sense. They made it seem like I asked for what I got, like I had forced their actions. I couldn't believe it. It was all lies to save their own behinds.

Prior to being transferred to the second hospital, I'd gotten wind that some of the local media had reported early on that I was the initiator, and that my family and I had taunted the other girls. I even called to the news stations to clear my name, but only one reporter responded. She wouldn't even take my statement, which would have given the true account. So of course hearing more fabrications sent anger surging through my veins. I let the prosecutor know the truth. He assured me that he already knew their version was made up. He'd prosecuted enough cases to see right through the lies and deceit, and was certain justice would prevail. I felt better hearing him tell me that, so I placed the upcoming trial in the back of my mind, and focused all my attention on finally going home.

In all honesty, there wasn't too much apprehension about going home, or what I would possibly face. I prayed constantly and thought a lot about faith. My faith in God and His ability to do all things paved my road that was to come. I knew my family would hold me down. I knew they'd back me up no matter what.

Also, through my newly created Instagram page, I began documenting my fight to recover. I wanted people to see that God is real and just how good He'd been to me. Through my photos, *everyone* was able to see what to expect regarding my physical appearance. I wasn't going to sugar coat it. If they accepted me, great and if not, it's their loss. I refused to dwell on appearance, or throw a pity party for myself. With my Instagram account, I was given a chance to jump right into accepting myself like I was jumping into a lake of cold water. I got over the initial freeze quickly instead of gradually stepping into it, taking my time to get used to my appearance.

The response to all of my Instagram updates and photos became a huge motivation for my future. It started off by receiving responses from family members and close friends. But as time passed and word of my page spread, my number of followers swelled. Before long, the photos of my recovery and my scars, no matter how brutal, seemed to inspire people. I began to get responses from people who were going through their own struggles; some just as bad as mine, others even worse. Each of them recited how they were now following my page almost religiously because of my transparency. They were constantly telling me I was their motivation to keep pushing through their own battles. Through my strength and courage, they were gaining their own.

I can't explain how it felt to be such an object of attention and inspiration. Obviously I didn't step out in front of that car that fateful night and say, "Hey, come run me over so I can be a lightning rod for inspiration!" That was never my intent. But to see my journey now making people strong enough to triumph over their own problems meant something special to me that I still can't quite describe. It was at that moment I figured out what my purpose on earth was.

God hadn't placed so many obstacles and hurdles in my life, including this one, for nothing. He'd done it all so I could become a testimony of perseverance that proves that no matter what your struggle or circumstances are, there's always a light at the end of it all.

My purpose was now crystal clear to me.

After four long months, I was finally wheeled out of the hospital in my wheelchair. Of course my mother, my right hand, came to pick me up. I can't begin to describe how it felt to finally be headed home. After being in the hospital for four months, it felt surreal to finally be able to go outside freely, and never turn back. It truly *did* feel like a new slate, a very new lease on life. I couldn't wait to get started.

Upon leaving, instead of going to my home, I had to move in with my mother because my electricity was off.

That obstacle, nor the fact that my finances were in shambles, affected me too much. I learned the hard way to take life's obstacles as they came, and deal with them head on. In my rehabilitative state, my mother wanted me near her anyway, so she could make sure I was okay at all times. I remember smiling, thinking, *I'm still grateful.*

The greatest thing about coming home for me was finally being able to be with my children every day, all day instead of just a few days out of the week. I had missed them terribly while I was in the hospital. I had worried about them constantly, no matter how much my family assured me they were okay and that they were being taken care of. I guess that's just the way mothers are built. Being disconnected from what we have given birth to is never something we can truly wrap our minds and hearts around. It's torture beyond words.

Along with my mother, my kids immediately pitched in to help out with my rehabilitation. They all did much more than their part. My mother and my daughter would bathe me, and help me do my self-catheterization, while my boys would lift me off the couch, carrying me wherever I needed to be. They were all my nurses, cooks, cleaners and therapists. They never let me out of their sight.

Having my children care for me felt a little strange in the beginning. It felt like it wasn't the natural order of things. Roles had been changed. Once upon a time I carried them to bed. Now they carried me. Once upon a time I held their arms out, guiding them, while they were learning how to walk. Now they held their arms out to me. It felt weird, but I got used to it. It's what you call unconditional love.

As word of me finally being home spread, certain friends and family dropped by to visit; some to give genuine words of encouragement and support, others just to see the damage. I have to admit *that* part of being home hurt. I learned who my real friends were. It became obvious that now that I was in a position where I couldn't be of service to certain people, I was of no use to them at all. Those people stopped by to say hello, and never stopped by again. It troubled me for a brief moment.

Believe me, it's difficult accepting that the people you would've given your right arm for wouldn't do the same for you when the chips are down. They wouldn't even donate their time. I realized I couldn't expect everyone to take my rehabilitation journey with me. As long as the *real* friends and *real* family stepped up, that's all that mattered.

Things were looking up. Eventually the lights in my home were cut back on, and I began to feel comfortable enough in my recovery process to move back in. Still, my mother remained closely involved, taking me to doctor's appointments, the grocery store, and wherever else necessary. My nephew, Cortez, was also a very big help. Since I didn't want to burden my children and still wanted them to enjoy their childhood, school functions, and mall visits with friends, he would stop by often to help out. My sister and certain other family members remained close and dependable also. Trina, a true friend, even took all of my children shopping for school clothes. My blessings flowed and my faith never wavered.

During this time, I also continued to remain active on my Instagram page. I continued to document my day-to-day recovery. My journey continued to be an inspiration to my followers. More and more people began to follow my account and give me words of encouragement while sharing their own experiences. Through their experiences, I gained even more strength to face my own. But despite my progress life began to show it had no compassion for my situation.

Life isn't a carrousel or a Ferris wheel with a conductor standing off to the side collecting tickets. You can't ask it to slow down or stop so you can get off when things become too difficult to bear. Life doesn't work that way. No matter what your situation, no matter how traumatic or hurtful, the landlord *still* wants his rent. The light company and gas company *still* want their monthly payments. And even death *still* comes calling.

My Uncle Butchie passed away. His death left me in shock. The two of us had grown super tight while I was in the hospital. He always came by to visit even though he was the type who *hated* hospitals. So when he came to visit me I knew he loved me.

When Butchie passed, obviously it shattered my mother's heart also. I felt terrible for her. She was helping me to survive my accident and in the process she lost both her mother and her brother. It hurt me so bad to see the despair in her eyes. But my mother continued pushing. I realized my strength must've been hereditary. My mother had passed her survivor traits onto me.

Moving back into my home, I was already behind on my bills and my rent. But my financial wreck grew much worse over time. Since I couldn't work, I had no income. The survivor's benefits and my new social security benefits from the accident helped, but that money wasn't even putting a dent in my monthly expenses. Imagine being a single parent with four children, along with current and past due bills due to the several months spent in the hospital. Life will get rough.

Another thing that caused my rent to fall behind was my oldest son's high school graduation. Obviously graduation was an important day for my baby and an important day for me too. After all, I ruined my chances of getting a high school diploma. But since money was tight, I had to choose between paying the rent that month or paying for his senior dues. Say what you want, but I did what I think *any* mother would've done in that situation.

I paid his senior dues.

Before long, I found myself four months behind on the rent and struggling. Eventually I was evicted. I continued to pray my heart out to God and kept my faith in Him. I knew no matter what, He would never place more on my back than I could handle. I never stopped believing that better days would come. Despite my prayers, although they gave me strength to keep pushing, trials and tribulations rained down.

After Butchie's funeral, my family was faced with another scare and Charmaine went into labor. My mother, India, and I went with her to the hospital. When we first arrived everything was going well. The beginning of her labor started with no problems. Suddenly things changed and Charmaine began to hemorrhage. As she did, the baby became stuck. When I looked over, I could see the baby's head literally dangling from inside of Charmaine. Her face turned blue. Then when I looked at Charmaine, her eyes began to uncontrollably roll in her head. Both my mother and India began to panic as the doctors and nurses scrambled about the room.

Instead of panicking, I chanted in a low voice, "Jesus, do your thing!" and as I continued to repeat it the doctors and nurses pulled my niece's lifeless body from Charmaine. She was whisked out of the delivery room for an immediate emergency operation. As all this was going on, I just continued to yell over and over again, "Jesus, do your thing!" I wouldn't stop. I wouldn't stay quiet. In my heart, I felt that my words wouldn't go unheard.

They didn't.

Both my niece and my sister survived.

My God is an awesome one. I don't doubt it. He's always there when I need Him. He's always there when times are darkest. I thank Him for that each day, several times a day. But now, I was going to need His help in giving me the strength to face the one woman who had made my life the darkest; the one who hit me.

At that point, my mind was focused on moving forward and overcoming situations. I learned through my tribulations that the devil doesn't know what to do with someone who refuses to give up. The driver of that car didn't kill me. She made me stronger.

FORGIVENESS IS A TRAIT OF THE STRONG

When someone changes your life for the absolute worst, what do you do when you see that person again? How do you react when you're placed in their presence again? What exactly registers when your eyes finally make contact? Do you react with vengeance? Or do you follow what God teaches about character?

On the outside of a situation looking in, everyone always says, "If it were *me*, I would've done this, or I would've done that." Everyone has their opinions on how they think they would react during an unfamiliar situation. I'm no different. I honestly thought I would lash out at the woman who ran me over when I finally saw her again. I thought the sight of her face would fill me with uncontrollable fury.

The first time I saw her was one morning at The Justice Center in Cleveland, Ohio. It was during one of many pre-trials. I was with my mother, my two oldest sons, and Cortez. We were getting on the elevator to leave because this particular pre-trial had been rescheduled. We hadn't even made it into the courtroom. As we were standing at the elevator, the floor, which was filled with dozens of people conversing, began to clear out. As we stood there, I noticed a man that the prosecutor had pointed out to me recently. The man was her lawyer. After noticing him, I also noticed a young woman standing beside him. The two were conversing and laughing. Looking at her much more closely, I assumed it was the woman who had hit me with the car.

While I was staring at the woman, the tragic night's events played back in my head. They literally rushed towards me in a flash like a linebacker towards a quarterback. They enveloped me. It was the first time I really thought about that night since finding the will to live. I wouldn't have recognized her if I hadn't seen her standing beside the lawyer. That surprised me because before that, I never would've ever expected to be so calm after seeing the person who had done so much damage to me. The mind is a funny thing, I guess.

As we all stood at the elevator literally within arm's reach of each other, she and her lawyer conversed and snickered. Her laugh was much louder than his. I can remember looking at her and wondering what right did she have to laugh about *anything*? What right did she have to find enjoyment in anything? It was like she didn't have a care or worry in the world. It registered that she moved on with her life during the past several months, not really caring about what I'd gone through.

174

While I stared at her, she glanced over at me. The glance was just that, a glance. She didn't look at me for more than a fraction of a second. There was no apology. There was no wave, or gesture to show remorse. She then continued on with her conversation as if she hadn't seen me, or as if she simply didn't give a damn. I can remember being amazed at the fact that a person could be that heartless. I just couldn't see myself being able to stand so close to someone I hurt and not feel anything. I couldn't see myself not having any compassion or remorse. It shocked me to see her lack those things. It still shocks me until this day.

During their conversation, the lawyer happened to look over at me. When he did, he immediately noticed who I was. He also, I'm assuming, got a chance to see his client's dirty work up close and personal. He gave me a wide-eyed look. It was an alarming look of surprise. I'll never forget it. The sight erased all laughter and smiles from his face. His expression and demeanor became professional. He didn't say a word to her from that point, although she kept right on talking as if everything was fine.

Honestly, I really wanted to do something horrible to her at that moment. Who wouldn't? She didn't deserve happiness. She didn't deserve to smile. She deserved the exact pain she inflicted on me. I wanted to see her hurt like she hurt me. I wanted to see her life change like she changed mine. If I wasn't in that wheelchair, who knows? Maybe I would have acted on those thoughts. At that moment, I simply chose to pull closer to God and fight off the ungodly feelings my flesh craved. I chose to pray for the strength to erase those thoughts from my mind, and those intentions from my heart. Two wrongs never make a right.

My mother, who is obviously a very soft-spoken person, wasn't as forgiving. She wanted a piece of her. It showed on her face. It showed in her eyes. She stared at the woman with a spiteful glare that I never witnessed from her before. It was then that I knew getting on that elevator with her and her lawyer would've been a mistake for all persons involved. In such a tight space and with the tempers of my mother, sons, and nephew flaring, someone would've been hurt very badly. The situation would've grown much worse than it already was.

Thankfully, I learned from the night we fought the young ladies in our driveway, that flaring tempers could lead to disastrous situations. It wasn't worth it. So instead of boarding the elevator when the doors opened, I locked the wheels of my wheelchair and told my family we would wait for the next one. Besides, I figured we would get our justice in court later on.

As months passed, there were more pre-trials and continuances. Before that, I never knew the judicial process took so long. I knew about arraignments and trials, but I never figured there would be other dates in between; they were countless and nerve racking. I saw no reason for so many of them.

Anyway, during yet another court session, the attorneys gathered me, and all of my family members who witnessed the incident, into a small room. As far as we knew, we were all supposed to go into court and basically tell everything that happened that night. I didn't want to have my family relive the incident. It was difficult for me to relive it and I felt strange about bringing them into it. Despite what I felt, it had to be done. After a tedious wait, the prosecutor came in and told us there would be no trial yet. The woman who hit me would be entering a plea the following week, which he assumed would be a guilty plea. Then, sentencing would be set for a later date.

It became frustrating, but my faith in the justice system remained. The following week rolled around. My family and I arrived at The Justice Center on time. We didn't want to miss a thing. As we sat in the courtroom waiting for the woman to give her plea, an entire hour passed. She was actually over an hour late for the proceedings. I couldn't believe it. Then when she finally showed up, she pranced into the courtroom with an attitude, as if her time was being wasted. She was truly the poster child for being disrespectful. Her attitude was evident as she leaned lazily against the post in front of her. It was like she really didn't take the court system, or what she had done seriously.

As the proceedings finally moved forward and she gave the judge her excuse for being late, she also told him that she was fearful for her life because she was scared of *my* family. Appalled, my blood boiled. Had she not learned anything from her previous actions?

The next few moments shocked me. She said, "The only reason I'm pleading guilty is because I need to get this over with and get back to my children in Florida."

Immediately, the lawyer leaned over to correct his client. Since it was a small courtroom and I was sitting less than ten feet behind them, I heard him say, "No Contest."

Instantly, she corrected herself, changing her plea to "No Contest."

Hearing her sudden plea change, and her carelessness, angered me. It was just like the moment we saw each other outside of the elevator. I couldn't believe there was a person walking around in this world with no sympathy for the people they hurt. It baffled me. She ran me over with a car, dragged me through the streets and never even apologized. Aren't we as human beings creatures of emotion? Don't we all have a conscience? How can a person turn them on and off? As a survivor of rape, molestation, and domestic violence, I came across some heartless folks in my time, but this took the cake!

Despite my allegiance to God, I have to admit, my thoughts at that moment were horrible.

God taught me so much during my tumultuous journey and my walk with Him. One of the things He taught me was that it's never good to hold onto resentment, spite, or hatred. As long as you do, the person you have those feelings for has control over you. The only way to take away that control is to forgive them. It's difficult, but it's the only way.

The moment I saw her at the elevator, I forgave her. But as time passed, my forgiveness was continuously tested by her selfishness. Her immaturity and coldness made me want to snap. It made me want to see her burn in hell. But one of the most unlikely people was about to place the concept of forgiveness into perspective for me.

My cousin Ernie is in his fifties. He's one of those old-school men who takes the concept of family and retribution very seriously. He wasn't about games. He'd

lost his sister to the Cleveland streets recently. She'd
been murdered. Her death left him filled with something
beyond anger. I knew he was the type to erupt at any
moment.

Shortly after the woman issued her plea, the judge
asked my family if there was anything we wanted to say.
I was too shaken and angry to speak. My family's
tempers were flaring. I didn't want them to speak
because I knew the situation in the courtroom could get
violent. Within seconds, Ernie stood. My body trembled
as he headed to the front of the courtroom. I just *knew*
he was going to do something to her. When he reached
the front of the courtroom and stood at the podium, he
was only a few yards away from her.

The entire room was silent.

"What you did was reckless," my cousin began as he
looked over at her, never blinking or allowing his eyes to
stray away from her. "You turned our entire family
upside down. But we're a strong family. We've been
through a lot, a number of tragedies. But this one was
one of the hardest. We spent countless days up at the
hospital with my cousin, not knowing if she was going to
live or die. Now, as if what you did to her didn't mean
anything, you have the nerve to stand yourself up here
and talk about walking the beaches of Florida while my
cousin has no idea if she'll ever walk again?"

All eyes were on her.

"You've got the nerve to talk about wanting to see
your children when you almost took her away from *hers*?"

She said nothing.

I thought Ernie was going to snap. I could see it in
him. I could see his rage building. The bailiffs weren't

going to be able to get to him quick enough, I knew. He was going to hurt her.

What he did next surprised me.

He surprised us all.

"Despite everything you've done," he told her. "We as a family forgive you."

I was stunned.

"And I hope that you find God along the way and repent for what you did," he continued. "I really do."

We were speechless. We couldn't believe that had just come from Ernie. But as I said, he placed forgiveness into perspective for me. I figured if one of the hardest men God had ever placed on this Earth could forgive, I could too. As my cousin headed back to his seat, I felt so proud of him. I loved him more than ever.

In that moment, I had no idea how much disappointment and let down we were all headed for.

∝ **CHAPTER 18** ∽

FAITH

*What a difference time, effort, fight and FAITH
can make! Anything is possible if you just fight
for what you want and what you believe in. When
I was in that wheelchair I knew that one day I
would walk again. I had FAITH in God that if
I kept on fighting, He would do the rest.*

Ebony's Life Lesson #19

A PURPOSE-FILLED LIFE

Obviously disappointment and let down have been an almost continuous cycle in my life. I've experienced it at its most extreme levels from childhood up until now. It never seemed to be far behind at any moment of my life. I finally learned to embrace it. I embraced it because it couldn't be ignored. Each disappointment was obviously preparing me for something greater in life. The disappointment and let down I was about to face was going to be one of the most difficult to embrace.

After my cousin spoke on my family's behalf, the judge found the woman who hit me guilty of Aggravated Vehicular Assault, a lighter charge than I expected. It disappointed me but I accepted it. The judge then set a date for sentencing. I prayed about it, and left that battle for The Lord.

On the sentencing day, I prayed hard to God that justice would be served. Up until that moment, I was told that Aggravated Vehicular Assault was a charge where probation was an option. That made no sense to me. She basically tried to kill me. How could that warrant probation? I also discovered she had been convicted of Menacing and Assault a few years prior, so it was obvious this wasn't the first time she felt she could inflict violence on someone. She had gotten off on probation for that conviction. Still though, I had my faith in God.

Up until sentencing, I had been praying just as hard as before. I had even asked my social media family to pray for me also. I didn't want to leave anything to chance. Sitting with me in the courtroom were my two older sons, my mother, India, Darnell's mother and several of my cousins. On the other side of the courtroom was my attacker and several of her family members. Along the sides of the courtroom were several sheriffs. Strangely, I sat in between my family and her family in my wheelchair in the aisle. As we sat there waiting for the proceedings to begin, the prosecutor reminded me that Aggravated Vehicular Assault meant probation could possibly be the outcome.

The judge finally entered the courtroom from her chambers and sat down. Before she imposed sentencing, she asked if my family would like to say anything. We were advised that we could only speak on why the defendant deserved jail time, not what actually happened that night. India was the first to speak. She read a letter she had written. When she was done, it was my turn. My mother wheeled me to the front of the courtroom. Once up front, I read a letter I had written too. From it, I mentioned that my attacker knew in her heart the real events of what happened that night. She knew I was the peacemaker in the situation. She knew what she had done was inhumane and unprovoked. Most importantly, she knew that I was underneath that car as she dragged me. She could hear my family screaming for her to stop. She could see them in her rearview mirror. She simply chose not to stop.

Openly, I also said that I wasn't sure why she was only being given a charge of Aggravated Vehicular Assault. It was far too lenient, for such a heinous crime. Whatever the reason, I practically begged that she be given the harshest sentence possible. I practically pleaded that she wouldn't be allowed to walk out of that courtroom a free woman. My children already lost their father. Now this woman had attempted to take their mother too. She had to be held accountable for what she did.

When I was finished, my mother-in-law wheeled me back beside my family. The judge then asked my attacker to come to the front of the courtroom and speak. We watched her as she took every step. When she finally reached the podium, she began to speak. From the moment she opened her mouth, there was no remorse or truth. She lied consistently about what happened that night, and her reasons for what she had done. Among other things, she said she ran me over by accident and out of fear for her own life. She said we were attacking her with baseball bats. She even went as far as to say my cousin Ernie, who was in the hospital the night of the incident battling Lupus, actually pulled her out of the car and beat her. I couldn't believe it. If that were true, why not take the case to trial? Nothing but lie after lie continued to spew from her mouth. There wasn't a single word of truth. She even said she didn't know she hit me.

Staring at her back, I was furious. Once again it was just so difficult to believe and accept that a person could be that way. It was like she had ice coursing through her veins. To top it off, when she was finished speaking, she turned to me and said 'Sorry' with the nastiest tone. There was nothing genuine about it. She didn't even look me in the eye as she said it. She simply turned, spat the word, and turned back to face the judge.

I along with my family grew more furious not only with her lies and her nasty attitude, but also the fact that she was being allowed to speak almost in entirety about the events of that night while we were told before that we could only speak on why she should be sentenced. It wasn't fair. It was like I was being railroaded. The sentencing seemed like a one-sided trial. I immediately let my lawyer know. I refused to bite my tongue. My family did the same. We had gotten so verbally livid one of the sheriffs had to intervene. The prosecutor had to intervene also. I asked him what was going on. Why was this being allowed to happen? He basically told me this was part of the sentencing process. I told him that I didn't feel it was fair. If she could tell her version of what happened that night, then it should be only right that I tell mine. I might as well have been talking to the air though. I wasn't allowed to say anything else.

As I sat there seething as her sister was allowed to speak. Just like the girl who hit me, she gave her own version of the events. Of course her version was laced with lies also but she actually showed remorse. She actually cried. She actually turned to me, apologized and said that she wished with all her heart that night hadn't happened. She said she really was sorry about what had happened to me. As I looked in her face and her eyes, I could see her pain. I could see her hurt. In all honesty, I believe her tears were genuine. Still though, I could only shake my head at her because her apology, no matter how sincere and heartfelt, had been preceded by just as many of her lies as her sister's.

Sitting there that entire time was difficult. I felt like I was being violated. I felt like that dreadful night was happening all over again. In addition, more bailiffs and sheriffs had now entered the room. I assumed it wouldn't end well.

After what seemed like forever, the judge was finally ready to announce sentencing. There wasn't a word spoken or even a sound of someone shuffling in their seat. Then just like a sledgehammer had hit me directly in the chest, after a brief tongue-lashing from the judge, I heard the words, "five years probation," fall from her mouth. I was in utter disbelief. Seconds later, I wheeled myself out of the courtroom into the hall. I couldn't stand to be in there for even one more second.

As my children and several of my family members joined me in the hall, I felt defeated. I just couldn't believe I was being violated once again. It was truly a dark moment for me and one that I will never ever forget. I was so hurt. Tears fell from my eyes. My heart shattered. My soul ached. What hurt me the most was seeing Darnez's tears. It reminded me of the moment where he cried terribly at his father's funeral. It's a shame people don't realize how one event can tear down a family.

As the girl's family exited the courtroom, there was nothing but smiles on their faces, including on the face of the girl who hit me with the car. What had been done to me was now the furthest thing from their minds. Justice for me meant absolutely nothing to them.

To prevent drama and violence, the sheriffs were careful to stay between my family and theirs. They remained there until her family got on the elevator and went on about their lives. After the elevator doors closed, among disappointed words of my family, I could only sit in silence. There was nothing I could say. There was nothing I could do except hurt. Then my oldest son, Darnell knelt in front of me, looked up into my eyes and asked softly, "Ma, why are you crying? Don't we believe in God?"

Those words sunk in immediately.

Wiping away my tears, he said, "God is going to take care of it. He's not going to let her get away with it. He's got us."

I realized my baby was right. His words inspired me. I thanked God for using my son's voice to get His message across. Whatever God's reason for letting things turn out the way they did, would soon be revealed on His time. In the end, there would be justice. That's the type of God He is. With that realization, I never cried about what happened in that courtroom again. Knowing God will eventually handle it in His own time, I placed it all in His hands and moved on. From that point, I took all my anger and fury and placed it into my fight to get completely well, and desire to build a better future for myself and my children.

.

CHAPTER 19

BLANK POSSIBILITIES

*Time heals all wounds but you have to let go of
blank possibilities and "what if's". Holding on is
doing nothing but delaying your healing process!
Let go so that your wounds can begin to heal.*

Ebony's Life Lesson #20

THE JOURNEY BEGINS

It's funny how sometimes a child's words can have
such an impact. A few days after the court case my son's
words continued to ring in my head. "Ma, why are you
crying? Don't we believe in God? He's gonna take care
of it!" It made me reflect on just how much God had
actually taken care of me. It caused me to reflect on each
situation that He had delivered me from, and the
strength to get through each ordeal.

Thankful that the court process was finally over and
my emotional roller coaster ride had ended, I was ready
to close that chapter of my life. But I knew that in order
to do that, I would have to forgive the woman who'd
intentionally run me down, changing my life forever. I
knew that the inability to stop resenting her would only
plant a poisonous seed in my heart; a seed that would
only grow into a bitter and angry plant, releasing toxic
fumes throughout my body. I'd come so far, wanting to

live, there was no way I'd allow myself to slowly die on the inside, contaminating those around me. Living with anger and revenge in my heart, while my attacker went on with her life, didn't make much sense.

I have always been the type of person to take responsibility for the things I've done in life. I'd learned not to take responsibility for other's wrong doings, and even though I felt like the driver never took full responsibility for what she'd done, I still forgave her. She had actually fueled the journey ahead of me. You see, forgiveness isn't necessarily for the person who wronged you. Forgiveness is for you. It allows you to be free of the pain, heartache, bitterness and misery that comes along with not pardoning their actions. After all, Ephesians 4:32 says, "Be kind to one another, tenderhearted, forgiving one another, as God in Christ forgave you."

If the words from the good book don't make you understand, try this: not forgiving is like letting someone live rent free in your head. Deep inside, I knew that if the Lord could forgive me for all of the things I'd done in my past, I had to forgive countless people.

I started with Shawn. Even though I told myself, I had forgiven him long before my traumatic car accident, he called one day out of the blue and apologized. "Eb, I'm sorry for all that I put you through. I was young and drinking and didn't know any better. I know I took you through a lot and I'm sorry."

His words soothed my soul because I knew that he found peace within himself and asked for forgiveness from God for what he had done to me. I'm not justifying men putting their hands on women, or vice-versa, but people can change and repent for their mistakes. Shawn had obviously turned his life around. We were even co-parenting in a positive way, and became very good friends. I truly believe that something went wrong in his life that caused him to do the things he'd done. Damaged people tend to damage others. Luckily, I'd grown since our days together. Between maturing and knowing God's word, it was easy to forgive Shawn.

Luke 6:37 tells us, "Judge not, and you will not be judged; condemn not, and you will not be condemned; forgive and you will be forgiven."

Honoring my heavenly father's words, I even forgave the family member who molested me and. Although neither of us have ever said a word to one another about those instances, it's clear that the constant drug use played a part in his actions. I don't condone any of it, but I can move on from it without malice in my heart. In fact, when I frequently see him, I'm able to offer encouraging words to keep him on the right track. I see the shame in his eyes and I take that as his apology. I didn't need anything else.

Then, there's the man who raped me in the bathroom of my aunt's home. I'd held onto my angry feelings toward him for years. It took more time than expected to forgive him, but rightfully so. I actually saw him at a fourth of July fireworks show years after the rape, walking with a female. He looked like a deer caught in headlights. Strangely, I didn't want him dead. I simply prayed for him.

God was certainly working on a new me.

I know someone reading this will find it difficult to understand. Forgiveness isn't an easy topic and many find it hard to do. But for me, if I don't forgive people who have wronged me, then I am wrong too. When we ask for forgiveness from God, it's granted because of the blood of Jesus, so why can't we forgive someone who has fallen into sin just as we have? Remember, circumstances can change at any time. One day, someone may have to forgive you for an awful thing that you've done.

Besides, it's so much easier on your spirit. Replace the anger and bitterness caused by the things others have done to you with love and affection. "Be ye kind, one to another."

Unknowingly, every wrong that has ever been committed against us matures us in some way. Personally, I'm not happy about the countless misfortunes in my life, yet I now realize they each had a hand in leading me to my purpose; a purpose that I've been prepped for my entire life! Gaining strength and wisdom from each situation I've been through, good or bad, has been a plus, preparing me for my calling. And every mistake made contained a lesson to be learned. My purpose has been personally written for me and carefully planned out by Jehovah himself. It's something that I must do.

Proudly, I say that my purpose is to show people the healing hands of God, step-by-step, and that he does answer prayers. My purpose is to give the nonbeliever a reason to believe, to give the person on the fence a reason to hop over, and to give the believer a reason to say, "I told you so!"

EBONY CANION

My purpose on this Earth is to reach out to those who are depressed, lost, or have been dealt a death sentence due to a health challenge; to uplift the women and men who need to hear that they are somebody; to inspire people to have the courage to be different and embrace who they are; to show the person who has been through a tragic situation that you can still have joy through pain, and that you too have a purpose.

I have to show people that S.C.A.R.S are beautiful and that they symbolize a Strong Courageous And Remarkable Survivor! I have to motivate people and give them a reason not to give up, a reason not to complain, and a reason to stop judging people based on their looks!

That woman or man who has no hair may be battling cancer, or could be a cancer survivor. That person in the wheelchair was an innocent bystander and is fighting to cope with his or her reality! That guy who has a prosthetic leg lost it during a war, fighting for our country! The timid and closed off lady is hiding her pain and scars from her abuser! The girl who you think is a geek is simply trying to be the first in her family to graduate! The girl who you call a whore has been molested and thinks sex is the only way to a man's heart! The young child who looks different was simply born with Downs Syndrome and is the sweetest kid you'll ever meet, and that woman who is scarred from head to toe, who has braces and walks with a cane, has overcome adversity.

Those people are all survivors just like me and together we're all headed on a journey to touch the world!

❧ **CHAPTER 20** ❧

MY PAST IS MY PAST

My past is my past and I thank my past for the lessons I have learned. My past gives me strength to live in my present and my present gives me hope for my future. My steps are paved in front of me for a reason; therefore, I will not walk backwards! My destiny is ahead!

Ebony's Life Lesson #21

EBONY CANION: A TRUE SURVIVOR

Reflecting on my past, I see life so clearly now. Things that I thought mattered, all of a sudden didn't, and things that I took lightly now mean the world to me. Surviving such a traumatic situation changed me.

I now see the world through loving and forgiving eyes. My past is my past and cannot be changed, but ultimately it can be learned from. Of course there were some good times, but oddly, most of us remember our bad times even more. For me, it seems as if I've been to hell and back, but I refuse to look back on my failures as regrets, because they were necessary. They made me who I am today. If you don't fail, how can you learn? I've learned a lot!

If I knew back in my teenage years that having sex would have such an impact, I wouldn't have done it. I truly believed sex was what I was supposed to give a man in exchange for attention. I also thought sex was something that wasn't to be treasured. I had no clue how much my body was worth spiritually.

I wish someone had taught me to treasure my body and to hold out for someone who I would spend the rest of my life with. I dropped a piece of my mind, body and soul off with every man that I'd ever slept with. Because of this, I was missing important pieces of myself as I went through life, pieces that I can never get back! I want to encourage the youth to not rush into things. Boys and girls will still be there when the time is right.

If I knew then what I know now, I wouldn't have moved from house to house. I realize that I never gave my children the stability that they deserved. It wasn't fair for them to have to continuously make new friends, or be the new student at every school, but I didn't realize that in my younger years.

Also, the cost of moving put me in such a financial bind. There has to be a solid foundation in place for families, and continuous moving did not provide that for my children. Find a way to create a stable home for yourself, and for your family. Make it work where you are until you can get to where you want to be.

If I knew then what I know now, on that horrible night when I was hit by that car, I would've refrained from arguing with those girls. I would've explained to my family members that when tempers flare, there's no telling how things will end. To this day, I do believe some things should have been handled differently. We didn't have to argue back. Yes, they were in our driveway at 2 o'clock in the morning, refusing to pull out, but after they parked across the street, maybe my sister should have let them trespass in someone else's yard. We could've gone in the house instead of feeding into their ignorance. But an uncontrolled temper and a lack of better judgment combined can be a terrible thing.

It's something that I saw this night, and that I see far too often on reality TV, women fighting and arguing with one another. It may make for great entertainment for some, but it didn't have a great outcome for me. When someone has a temper that's out of control, it's easy to feed into it, but it takes a strong willed person to simply walk away. We absolutely have to think before we act because if we don't the outcome can be life changing for us as well as someone else.

If I knew then what I know now, I would've carefully chosen the people I hung around. The saying goes, 'you are the average of the top ten people you hang around.' It's true. Look around. If your circle of friends drink and smoke often, or party at least four nights a week, chances are you're mimicking some of their actions.

In my life I admittedly haven't been a good judge of character. I hung with the wrong people, nearly drank myself into oblivion, and let more of the negative things I saw people do rub off on me. This caused me to get wrapped up with the wrong crowd and make poor decisions. Whether it was the decision to gang bang, sell drugs, have casual sex, smoke weed or attempt to numb myself with alcohol. Either way, they were all wrong decisions!

Now I know the importance of acting with integrity and good character at all times is crucial, and something I teach to my children regularly.

If I knew then what I know now about change and how much good it would have done for me, I wouldn't have allowed myself to be so full of fear. Change was one of my biggest fears, but one of my biggest needs. The fear of changing some situations that were no good to me were on one side of the fence, and on the other side was a brand new beginning that could have shown me just what living really was!

If I knew then what I know now, my relationships with men would have been healthier. When I was with Shawn, we were two lost souls trying to lead one another down foggy paths. He was hurt and I was hurt too; therefore, I stayed in an unhealthy relationship. Two lost people will never know how to lead the other in the right direction! I allowed his abuse to continuously happen only because I was broken at the time.

Since then, I've learned that what we allow to happen to us is going to continue. I've also learned that if you don't completely love yourself and know where you're headed in life, failure is certain. You have to love yourself enough to know that sometimes it's okay to be alone in order to find yourself and then once you know who you are, you can add to the life of someone else. Ladies, you don't have to have a man to be happy. And now that I know this, I am at peace.

In short, I cheated death, broke up with all of my setbacks, got engaged to faith, and am now married to my bright future. Even though I haven't gotten back to perfect health, I'll never lose faith. Most people will read this book or follow my journey on Instagram and say, "Oh my God, look at her pictures. Look how her face was distorted. Look at what they did to her. She will never be the same again."

Lies. All Lies.

Don't look at my hospital photos and have sympathy for me. Look at those pictures of me down and out and say, "Wow, she overcame. She survived. Ebony Canion is a true survivor.

I may have been Left For Dead on that cold concrete on June 30, 2012, but today I live to encourage others. I'm standing strong, motivating people, continuing rehabilitation, and one day soon I will walk all by myself again.

ABOUT THE AUTHOR

Ebony Canion is an inspiration to everyone around her, despite the adversity she has faced throughout both childhood and adulthood. In fact, her countless traumatic experiences have molded her to be strong, resilient, and faithful, in short a survivor.

On June 30, 2012, her strength was tested more than ever before. Ebony was run over, then dragged for almost two hundred feet. She sustained multiple serious injuries and was in a coma for nearly two months. But keeping with the pattern of her life, Ebony's spirit of faithfulness was bent but never broken.

And it was then, healing in the hospital, that Ebony decided to share her story with the world. She had to learn how to walk, talk, and even eat again. As an inspiration to all who know her, Ebony's will to overcome, more importantly to survive, is unparalleled. Ebony, a role model to all, wants to show people all over the world that despite your scars your journey and disappointments they tell a story.

No matter how hard her life gets, she remains positive and faithful that God will see her through. Even when suffering, she puts everyone before herself. If you or someone you know wants to hear Ebony share her story in person, please contact us at lcbinfo2013@gmail.com.
For more information visit us online at:
www.lifechangingbooks.net
Twitter & Instagram: @survival_story
Facebook: www.facebook.com/survivalstory
www.thesurvivalstory.org

ABOUT THE PUBLISHER

Life Changing Books, more affectionately known as LCB, established in 2003, has become one of the most respected independent Trade Publishers amongst chain stores, vendors, authors and readers. LCB offers a variety of literature including, non-fiction, contemporary fiction, urban/street literature, and a host of other categories.

For more information visit us online at:
www.lifechangingbooks.net

Follow us on:
Twitter: @lcbooks
Instagram: @lcbooks
Facebook: www.facebook.com/LCBooks